THE HAMBURG RULES
FROM HAGUE TO HAMBURG VIA VISBY

SECOND EDITION

BY

CHRISTOF LÜDDEKE
FNI, ACIArb, MM

AND

ANDREW JOHNSON
Solicitor

LLP

LONDON NEW YORK HAMBURG HONG KONG
LLOYD'S OF LONDON PRESS LTD
1995

Lloyd's of London Press Ltd.
Legal & Business Publishing Division
27 Swinton Street
London WC1X 9NW
Great Britain

USA AND CANADA
Lloyd's of London Press Ltd.
Suite 308, 611 Broadway
New York, NY 10012, USA

GERMANY
Lloyd's of London Press GmbH
59 Ehrenbergstrasse, 22767 Hamburg
Germany

SOUTH-EAST ASIA
Lloyd's of London Press (Far East) Ltd.
Room 1101, Hollywood Centre
233 Hollywood Road
Hong Kong

First edition 1991
Second edition 1995

British Library Cataloguing in Publication Data
A catalogue record for this book
is available from the
British Library

ISBN 1-85044-884-1

Text set in 10/12pt Times by
Action Typesetting Limited, Gloucester
Printed in Great Britain by
WBC Print Limited
Bridgend, Mid-Glamorgan

PREFACE

No fanfare attended the coming into force of the Hamburg Rules on 1 November 1992 and most commentators still doubt whether the principal aims of the Convention, i.e. of improving upon the Hague Rules and promoting greater international uniformity, have been or will be realised. The figures on uniformity make interesting reading. The Hague Rules (the International Convention for the Unification of Certain Rules of Law Relating to Bills of Lading, 1924) entered into force in 1931, and to date there are 91 Contracting Parties, of which 19 are Contracting Parties to the Visby Protocol.

The Hamburg Rules were open for signature until 30th April 1979, by which time the Convention was signed, subject to ratification, by 27 States.

The Rules have now been in force since 1 November 1992 and a brief summary of the present situation amongst those States who have ratified is as follows:

- Chile, which ratified the Hamburg Rules on 9 July 1992, recently gave consideration to denouncing them. An inter-parliamentary committee of the Chilean Government concluded that denunciation would be premature given the short time the Rules have been in force. The Committee recommended that the matter be reviewed if it transpired that Chile's adherence to the Rules hindered its foreign trade.
- Egypt has deferred denunciation of the Hague-Visby Rules for the maximum allowed of five years. In the meantime Egypt will apply the Hamburg Rules only to carriage to or from other Hamburg Rule Contracting States.
- Kenya, Nigeria, Romania and Zambia are understood not to be applying the Rules, notwithstanding their ratification.

We understand that the Governments of France and Italy have authorised ratification of the Hamburg Rules although both States at present continue to apply the Hague-Visby Rules and the SDR protocols.

A round-up elsewhere reveals the following picture:

- The Canadian Carriage of Goods by Water Act 1993 adopting the Hague-Visby Rules came into force on 6 May 1993.
- The new Chinese Maritime Code which came into force on 1 July 1993 has substantially adopted the Hague-Visby Rules with some principles of the Hamburg Rules.

- In 1992, the Indian Carriage of Goods by Sea Act 1925 was amended to substantially adopt the Hague-Visby Rules.
- The Hague-Visby Rules entered into force in Japan on 1 June 1993 with the full support of both Japanese shipowners and shippers.
- Korea's Revised Commercial Code, which replaced the 1962 version, was introduced effective 1 January 1993. The provisions relating to the Carriage of Goods by Sea substantially adopt the Hague-Visby Rules. There is, however, no weight-based alternative to the package limitation of 500 SDR per package or shipping unit.
- The Hague-Visby Rules were incorporated into the Netherlands Code of Commerce and came into force on 26 July 1992.
- The Thailand Carriage of Goods by Sea Act BE2534 (1991) is substantially based on the Hague-Visby Rules and came into force on 23 February 1992.
- The Australian Carriage of Goods by Sea Act 1991 provided that the Hamburg Rules would automatically come into effect in Australia on 31 October 1994 unless the Government agreed to defer their application for a further three years. In fact the Government (upon advice from the Department of Transport and Communications) decided to take this option and postponed the coming into force of the Hamburg Rules until 1997. Recent indications suggest the possibility that any new Act is likely to be a mixture of provisions from the Hague-Visby Rules and the Hamburg Rules.

These developments rather confirm the continuing lack of enthusiasm for the Hamburg Rules amongst the international community and it remains the case that the cherished goal of uniformity in this field remains as elusive as ever.

In this second edition, as in the first, we approach the subject on the assumption that the reader will have some familiarity with the Hague and Hague-Visby Rules. We have given greater emphasis to the distinctions between the Hague, Hague-Visby and Hamburg Rules and have included in the Appendix a guide indicating the main differences between these codes.

We would like to express our thanks to Andrew Waldron of Hill Taylor Dickinson for his welcome and informed assistance in up-dating this edition.

Geneva, 11 February, 1995

CHRISTOF LÜDDEKE
ANDREW JOHNSON

TABLE OF CONTENTS

TABLE OF CASES

TABLE OF LEGISLATION

References in **bold type** are to sections where the text of the legislation is set out.

TABLE OF HAMBURG RULES

(United Nations Convention on the Carriage of Goods by Sea 1978)

References in **bold type** are to sections where the text of the rule is set out.

CHAPTER 1

THE HAMBURG RULES: UNITED NATIONS CONVENTION ON THE CARRIAGE OF GOODS BY SEA 1978

PREAMBLE

THE STATES PARTIES TO THIS CONVENTION

HAVING RECOGNISED the desirability of determining by agreement certain rules relating to the carriage of goods by sea,

HAVE DECIDED to conclude a Convention for this purpose and have thereto agreed as follows:

PART I. GENERAL PROVISIONS

Article 1. Definitions

In this Convention:

1. "Carrier" means any person by whom or in whose name a contract of carriage of goods by sea has been concluded with a shipper.

2. "Actual carrier" means any person to whom the performance of the carriage of the goods, or part of the carriage, has been entrusted by the carrier, and includes any other person to whom such performance has been entrusted.

3. "Shipper" means any person by whom or in whose name or on whose behalf a contract of carriage of goods by sea has been concluded with a carrier, or any person by whom or in whose name or on whose behalf the goods are actually delivered to the carrier in relation to the contract of carriage by sea.

4. "Consignee" means the person entitled to take delivery of the goods.

5. "Goods" includes: live animals; where the goods are consolidated in a container, pallet or similar article of transport or where they are packed, "goods" includes such article of transport or packaging if supplied by the shipper.

6. "Contract of carriage by sea" means any contract whereby the carrier undertakes against payment of freight to carry goods by sea from one port to another; however, a contract which involves carriage by sea and also carriage by some other means is deemed to be a contract of carriage by sea for the purposes of this Convention only in so far as it relates to the carriage by sea.

7. "Bill of lading" means a document which evidences a contract of carriage by sea and the taking over or loading of the goods by the carrier, and by which the carrier undertakes to deliver the goods against surrender of the document. A provision in the document that the

goods are to be delivered to the order of a named person, or to order, or to bearer, constitutes such an undertaking.

8. "Writing" includes, *inter alia*, telegram and telex.

Articles 1.1 and 1.2

One of the main features of the Convention is to draw a distinction between a "carrier" and an "actual carrier". The "carrier" is the person who enters into a contract of carriage with the shipper. The "actual carrier" is the person to whom the actual carriage of the goods has been entrusted. In many instances the carrier will himself perform the carriage as, for example, where a liner operator accepts cargo direct from a shipper. In such a case the liner operator will be the "carrier", there being no delegation of carriage by him to an "actual carrier". Conversely, where the carrier sub-contracts all or part of the carriage to another person, that person becomes an "actual carrier" within the meaning of the Convention. By virtue of Article 10 the carrier remains primarily responsible for the entire carriage, notwithstanding any delegation, while the actual carrier is jointly and severally liable for that part of the carriage which he undertakes.

A common example would be that of a time-charterer who contracts directly with the shipper but who entrusts the actual carriage of the goods to the shipowner. Here the "carrier" is the time-charterer and the "actual carrier" is the shipowner. It is useful to consider how the distinction between "carrier" and "actual carrier" applies to the following different types of bills of lading commonly used:

1. Owner's standard form bill signed by the master.
2. Owner's standard form bill of lading signed by an agent "for and on behalf of the owner or master.
3. Time-charterer's bill of lading signed by the master or "owner's agents".
4. Bills of lading on time-charterer's standard form signed on behalf of the time-charterer by his agent.[1]

In 1 to 3 it is almost certainly the case that the contracting carrier will be the owner of the vessel on whose behalf the port agents or master will be treated as acting in signing the bills. Thus the actual and contractual carrier, at least where the governing law is English, are likely to be the same.

Where, as in the fourth example above, time-charterers' bills of lading are signed by agents "on behalf of" time-charterers, it is likely that the contracting carrier will be the time-charterer[2]. It is only in this case that the performing and contractual carrier may be different. The owner will be the "actual carrier" and the time-charterers the (contractual) "carrier".

It is noteworthy that the Convention Relating to the Carriage of Passengers and their Luggage by Sea, more commonly referred to as the Athens Convention 1974

1. *Uniform Customs and Practice for Documentary Credits*, 1993 Revision, ICC Publication No 500.
2. *Gadsden* v. *Australian Coastal Shipping Commission* [1977] 1 NSWLR 575, New South Wales Court of Appeal.

distinguishes between, the contracting "carrier" and "performing carrier". The "performing carrier" as the name suggests puts emphasis upon the party performing the carriage and is defined as "the owner, charterer, or operator of a ship, who actually performs the whole or a part of the carriage". The definition of "actual carrier" in the Hamburg Rules is potentially wider than "performing carrier" under the Athens Convention although the focus of both is upon the party "performing" the carriage by sea.

It is commonly the case that a bill will contain a "demise clause" or "identity of carrier clause"[3] which attempts to identify the responsible (contractual) carrier. In most cases such clauses will attempt to make the owner or bareboat charterer of a vessel responsible. Such clauses are recognised by the English courts but not so in many other jurisdictions.[4]

The English courts have identified no conflict between the definition of "carrier" in the Hague Rules and such attempts to identify the responsible carrier on the reverse of bills of lading. However, in many countries an attempt to identify the carrier by use of such a provision on the reverse of a bill of lading is not recognised.[5]

Under the Hamburg Rules in cases 1 to 3 identified above a "demise clause" would have little practical effect, it merely states the obvious, i.e. that the owner or bareboat charterer is the carrier. Where, however, a bill of lading contains an "identity of carrier" clause, and is signed on a time-charterers' form by agents on behalf of time-charterers an attempt to identify the owners as the responsible carrier would offend against the provisions in the Hamburg Rules identifying the "actual carrier" as responsible.

Article 15 requires the bill of lading to identify the carrier and give his principal place of business. Surprisingly, there is no similar requirement to name the actual carrier save in cases of Through Carriage as set out in Article 11. Freight forwarders who issue their own "House" bill of lading will also be caught by the wide definition of "carrier" and indeed may also become "the shipper" given the wide terms of Article. 1.3.

Article 1.4

The consignee has not previously been defined in any of the other transport Conventions. It should be noted that Article 15 requires the inclusion of the

3. A typical identity of carrier clause would read: "If the ship is not owned by or chartered by demise to the Company or Line by whom this bill of lading is issued (as may be the case notwithstanding anything that appears to the contrary) this bill of lading shall take effect only as a contract with the owner or demise-charterer as the case may be as principal made through the agency of said Company or Line who acts as agents only and shall be under no personal liability whatsoever is respect thereof."

4. *The Berkshire* [1974] 1 Lloyd's Rep. 185, *Vikfrost* [1980] 1 Lloyd's Rep. 560, also upheld in Singapore, and see *The Grace Liberty* (1993) LMLN 362 Singapore Court of Appeal and in Japan by the Tokyo District Court in *The Jasmin* in 1990. *The Antares* (No. 2) [1987] 1 Lloyd's Rep. 424).

5. *The Newfoundland Coast* [1990] LMLN 271, US Court of Appeals.

consignee's name in the bill of lading but only if the consignee is named by the shipper.

Article 1.5

A notable change to the Hague/Hague-Visby Rules is the inclusion of "live animals" within the definition of "Goods". The carrier's responsibility for the carriage of "live animals" is, however, circumscribed by Article 5. It remains the case under the Hamburg Rules that deck cargo and animals are subject to special treatment.

Under the Hague/Hague-Visby Rules deck cargo is excluded from the definition of "Goods", where the goods are stated as being carried on deck in the bill and are so carried. It is noteworthy that the definition of "Goods" in the Hamburg Rules is not subject to this automatic exclusion. Thus, subject to the special provisions applicable to deck carriage under Article 9, the Hamburg Rules apply to cargo carried on deck.

Article 1.6

The definition of a "contract of carriage by sea" is wide enough to include any contract of affreightment although by Article 2.3 it is made clear that the Hamburg Rules are not compulsorily applicable to charterparties. As with the Hague/Hague-Visby Rules, it will remain open to the parties to agree (e.g. by the inclusion of a clause paramount) that the Hamburg Rules should have application under the terms of a charterparty.

Unlike the definition of "contract of carriage" in the Hague/Hague-Visby Rules the contracts to which the Hamburg Rules have application are not limited to bills of lading, or other "documents of title". In fact bills of lading are not mentioned at all in Article 1.6. Bills are certainly covered, as would be Sea Way Bills, and Combined Transport Bills (so far as the sea leg is concerned). Thus a carrier is not likely to be able to rely on lower limits of liability than those imposed by the Hamburg Rules, as was permitted by the English courts in a case[6] concerning the carriage of goods from Dover to Calais under a "commercial non-negotiable receipt", which stated that the Hague-Visby Rules should apply but set limits for carriers' liability below those applicable under the Rules. It was held that the Hague-Visby Rules did not apply compulsorily and the parties to the contract of carriage were therefore entitled to agree to lower limits.[7]

Where the contract is for the carriage of goods partly by land and partly by sea, for example carriage under a "combined transport bill of lading" or "through bill of lading", the rights and liabilities prescribed by the Convention will apply to the sea leg of the carriage only. Thus a through bill of lading carrier who undertakes pre-

6. *The Vechscroon* [1982] 1 Lloyd's Rep. 301.
7. But see *The European Enterprise* [1989] 2 Lloyd's Rep. 185.

carriage services (for example, the collection of goods from the premises of the shipper for delivery to the loading port), will be able to contract-out of liability for such services to the extent permitted under national law (or any applicable international convention, such as the CMR). The words "by sea" may give rise to difficulty. It is unclear whether carriage by inland waterways (rivers and lakes) is intended to be excluded. However, it would be unsatisfactory to apply a restrictive meaning and treat differently, for example, a carriage from Chicago to Sydney and a carriage from New York to Sydney.

Article 1.7

The bill of lading has not previously been defined in any of the transport Conventions. The definition includes any contract of affreightment although, as mentioned above, charterparties are specifically excluded by the operation of Article 2.3.

Article 1.8

It is suggested that a facsimile would also satisfy this definition. This is now a common method of communication and recognised as such.[8]

Article 2. Scope of application

1. The provisions of this Convention are applicable to all contracts of carriage by sea between two different States, if:
   (a) the port of loading as provided for in the contract of carriage by sea is located in a Contracting State, or
   (b) the port of discharge as provided for in the contract of carriage by sea is located in a Contracting State, or
   (c) one of the optional ports of discharge provided for in the contract of carriage by sea is the actual port of discharge and such port is located in a Contracting State, or
   (d) the bill of lading or other document evidencing the contract of carriage by sea is issued in a Contracting State, or
   (e) the bill of lading or other document evidencing the contract of carriage by sea provides that the provisions of this Convention or the legislation of any State giving effect to them are to govern the contract.

2. The provisions of this Convention are applicable without regard to the nationality of the ship, the carrier, the actual carrier, the shipper, the consignee or any other interested person.

3. The provisions of this Convention are not applicable to charterparties. However, where a bill of lading is issued pursuant to a charterparty, the provisions of the Convention

8. *Beatly* v. *First Exploration Funds, British Columbia*, 25 BCLR (2d) 377 (1988). and *Ralux NVSA* v. *Spencer Mason*, TLR 18 May 1989.

apply to such a bill of lading if it governs the relation between the carrier and the holder of the bill of lading, not being the charterer.

4. If a contract provides for future carriage of goods in a series of shipments during an agreed period, the provisions of this Convention apply to each shipment. However, where a shipment is made under a charterparty, the provisions of paragraph 3 of this article apply.

Article 2.1

The provisions of the Convention are applicable to all contracts of carriage by sea with the exception of charterparties. In practice, therefore, the Hamburg Rules will be applicable not only to bills of lading but also to Waybills, Short-Sea Notes, Express Bills of Lading and other similar contracts if they cover carriage between two States. One significant advance over the Hague/Hague-Visby regime is the mandatory application of the Convention to both inward and outward shipments from contracting states. The Rules also apply where the document evidencing the contract of carriage is issued in a contracting state or where the parties have agreed to their operation.

The original Hague Rules do not specify which voyages they are to apply to and it is a matter for a domestic court seized with a dispute to decide whether a carrier should be held responsible under the Hague Rules in respect of the subject voyage. Conversely, Article X applies the Hague-Visby Rules compulsorily to out-bound carriage solely. The Hamburg Rules apply to both in-bound and out-bound carriage.

Thus, for example, in the context of a voyage from England to Chile so far as the English courts are concerned the Hague-Visby Rules will have automatic application as a consequence of the Carriage of Goods by Sea Act 1971 (which applies the Hague-Visby Rules to outbound carriage from UK ports). The courts in Chile would be free to apply the Hamburg rules to in-bound carriage.[9] Such a situation would provide a "forum shopping" cargo owner with an interesting choice. Such a choice would be informed by some novel considerations, e.g. whether to seek the higher limits of liability provided by the Hamburg Rules, or in the case of unauthorised deck carriage seek to establish unlimited liability on the part of the carrier by suing under the Hague-Visby Rules.

It is common for a bill of lading to contain a "clause paramount" which will provide that the Hague Rules will govern the relationship between the carrier and the cargo owner unless the Hague-Visby Rules (or some other system of law) has compulsory application to the voyage in question. A clause paramount will be ineffective where the Hamburg Rules apply if the clause merely allows for the application of the Hague-Visby Rules in substitution for the contractually chosen Hague Rules, where the former have compulsory application.

Article 2.1 provides for the application of the Hamburg Rules where the contract of carriage is expressed to be subject to the Hamburg Rules (or the legislation of

9. It is, of course, the case that some European countries apply the Hague-Visby Rules to in-bound carriage. This is, however, an extension of the mandatory position under the Hague-Visby Rules.

any state giving effect to them). This wording is the same as that used in the Hague-Visby Rules.[10]

Under English law a statement in a bill of lading that the contract of carriage is subject to English law will not mean the automatic application of the Carriage of Goods by Sea Act 1971 and accordingly the Hague-Visby Rules.[11] It would, however, be a mistake to assume that a statement in a bill that the contract of carriage is to be conducted in accordance with e.g. Chilean law would not mean that the Hamburg Rules would apply.

Article 2.3, whilst excluding charterparties from the scope of the Convention, stipulates that the Rules do apply to bills of lading issued pursuant to a charterparty where the bill of lading is itself the contract of carriage. The position is the same under the Hague and Hague-Visby Rules.

A bill of lading issued for goods on a chartered ship represents the contract of carriage in the following circumstances:

1. Where the holder of the bill of lading is the shipper and the shipper is not the same person as the charterer; or
2. Where the shipper and the charterer are the same person and the bill of lading has been transferred to a third party. In this case the bill of lading represents the contract of carriage between the third party and the carrier.

Article 2.4 deals with contracts of carriage pursuant to which the carrier undertakes the future carriage of goods in a series of shipments during an agreed period. Such contracts are commonly called "Tonnage" or "Volume" contracts and are most frequently used for project cargo. The Hamburg Rules will apply to each shipment unless the shipment is made under a charterparty, in which case Article 2.3 operates.

The actual scope of application of the Hamburg Rules is limited to claims arising from loss of or damage to or delay of goods as defined by the Convention. In this sense they may not extend radically beyond the scope of the Hague Rules which have been given a wide interpretation by the English courts[12], at least where the courts have been asked to examine the effect of a "clause paramount" in a charterparty which has the effect of applying the Hague Rules to "cargo claims". In such circumstances the Hague Rules will tend to be applied except where the liabilities cannot reasonably be said to relate to cargo, e.g. speed and performance claims. It is certainly the case that the Hague Rules apply to the theft of cargo[13], as should be the case under the Hamburg Rules.

Article 3. Interpretation of the Convention

In the interpretation and application of the provisions of this Convention regard shall be had to its international character and to the need to promote uniformity.

10. Article 1(c).
11. *The Komninos S* [1991] 1 Lloyd's Rep. 370, CA.
12. *The Stena Pacifica* [1990] 2 Lloyd's Rep. 234.
13. *The Captain Gregos* [1989] 2 Lloyd's Rep. 63, but see *Kamil v. NPL* (1994) LMLN 382 Supreme Court of Victoria.

Article 3

An illustration of the broadly based and non-technical approach to be taken in interpreting the Convention demanded by Article 3 can perhaps be seen in the way in which the philosophy behind the rules is set out in Annex 2 in terms of a "common understanding" of the contracting parties.

It remains doubtful, however, whether Article 3 will achieve the object of promoting uniformity. The different legal systems of the Contracting States are certain to develop their own interpretation and case law on the Convention.

It may, be necessary to use wide-ranging materials to assist a court with the interpretation of the Convention, e.g. reference to decided cases in contracting countries may be appropriate, as may the *travaux preparatoires* (although the English courts have traditionally been reluctant to refer to the reasoning underlying legislation and Conventions).

PART II. LIABILITY OF THE CARRIER

Article 4. Period of Responsibility

1. The responsibility of the carrier for the goods under this Convention covers the period during which the carrier is in charge of the goods at the port of loading, during the carriage and at the port of discharge.

2. For the purpose of paragraph 1 of this article, the carrier is deemed to be in charge of the goods

(a) from the time he has taken over the goods from:

(i) the shipper, or a person acting on his behalf; or

(ii) an authority or other third party to whom, pursuant to law or regulations applicable at the port of loading, the goods must be handed over for shipment;

(b) until the time he has delivered the goods:

(i) by handing over the goods to the consignee; or

(ii) in cases where the consignee does not receive the goods from the carrier, by placing them at the disposal of the consignee in accordance with the contract or with the law or with the usage of the particular trade, applicable at the port of discharge; or

(iii) by handing over the goods to an authority or other third party to whom, pursuant to law or regulations applicable at the port of discharge, the goods must be handed over.

3. In paragraphs 1 and 2 of this article, reference to the carrier or to the consignee means, in addition to the carrier or the consignee, the servants or agents , respectively of the carrier or the consignee.

Article 4

The focus of the Hamburg Rules remains restricted to carriage of goods by sea. Interestingly, the United Nations Convention on International Multi Modal Transport concluded in 1980 applies many of the same principles regarding carriers' liability to combined transport where the issuer of a contract of carriage is responsible for land and sea legs. The Convention is not yet in force. It requires 30 contracting parties to accede to or ratify it.

Article 4 represents a considerable extension of the period for which the carrier is potentially liable over that under the Hague Rules. Article I of the Hague/ Hague-Visby Rules provides that the period of carriage is limited to "the period from the time when the goods are loaded on to the time they are discharged from the ship".

It may, however, be the case that a carrier can be liable under the Hague Rules for pre-loading liabilities (if they are incorporated into a charterparty). In a recent case,[14] the English Court of Appeal (in the context of charterparties incorporating US COGSA 1936) decided that a claim for pecuniary loss caused by a delay to loading (while tanks were cleaned) was time-barred under the Hague Rules as the claim related to the "loading" of goods.

It has been decided by the Supreme Court of British Columbia,[15] that the Hague Rules (under the Canadian Carriage of Goods by Water Act) did not apply to a period of three weeks during which goods were discharged at Singapore awaiting transhipment to their bill of lading destination. The court decided that this time did not qualify as a period during which goods were "carried by water". In this situation under the Hamburg Rules, the question would be whether the time the goods were waiting for transhipment was a period "during the carriage".

By Article 4 of the Hamburg Rules the responsibility of the carrier under the Convention is from "port to port". In other words, it covers the period whilst he is in charge of the goods at the port of loading, during the carriage and until the goods are delivered at the port of discharge. Under Article 4.2 the carrier is deemed to be in charge of the goods at the port of loading from the time he has taken them over from:

1. the shipper, or a person acting on his behalf; or
2. an authority or other third party to whom, pursuant to local law or regulation at the port of loading, the goods must be handed over for shipment.

The moment of "taking charge" by the carrier will undoubtedly vary from trade to trade.

In the Liner trade, taking charge would ordinarily occur when the carrier or his agent issues a delivery receipt or other similar document to the shipper or his representative at the loading port. In the bulk trade, the loading facility will not, in most cases, be under the control of the carrier and, therefore, neither the carrier nor his agent will usually be in a position to take over the goods until the loading process actually begins and the cargo is being loaded into the tanks of the ship.

Difficulties of interpretation may arise in circumstances where the carrier has taken over the goods from the shipper before they have reached the port of loading. For example, the carrier may take over the goods at the shipper's premises from which he has undertaken pre-carriage haulage to the port of loading. It is not clear

14. *The Ot Sonja* [1993] 2 Lloyd's Rep. 435.
15. *Captain* v. *Far Eastern Steamship Co* [1979] 1 Lloyd's Rep. 595.

whether Article 4.2(a)(i) extends the period of responsibility to the point at which the carrier takes over the goods at the premises of the shipper or whether Article 4.1 limits the period of responsibility to the point at which the goods arrive at the port of loading. It is submitted that the period of responsibility does not commence until the goods have arrived at the port of discharge notwithstanding any pre-carriage. However, a carrier may wish to protect himself by the use of an exemption clause that meets the requirements of Article 11.

Difficulties may also arise where the goods have been taken over by the agent of the carrier on arrival at the port of loading but are later damaged whilst in the custody of the port authority to whom the goods must be handed over for shipment pursuant to the regulations of the port. In such cases, the carrier will nevertheless be deemed to be in charge of, and therefore responsible for, the goods. The carrier might seek to regulate his position in the bill of lading by, for example, stipulating that he is not liable for the period of time during which the goods are in the compulsory custody of a third party at the loading or discharging port. However, any such clause in the bill of lading must not fall foul of the non-derogation provisions of Article 23.

Once the responsibility of the carrier has commenced under Article 4, all the subsequent ancillary operations (for example, shifting from the warehouse to the quay, loading, stowage, discharge, and shifting from the quay to the warehouse) will be an integral part of the contract of carriage and therefore the responsibility of the carrier.

The Convention contemplates delivery of the goods at the port of discharge by three separate mechanisms.

First, delivery is accomplished by handing over the goods to the consignee or his representative.

Secondly, in cases where the consignee does not receive the goods from the carrier, delivery is deemed to have taken place by the carrier placing the goods at the disposal of the consignee in accordance with the contract, local law or usage of the particular trade, applicable at the port of discharge. Thus, by placing the goods at the disposal of the consignee, the responsibility of the carrier under the Convention comes to an end without the need for acceptance by the consignee. This is an important right given to the carrier, enabling him to be relieved of his responsibility for the goods if the consignee does not fulfil his obligation to take delivery. However, it is unlikely that the carrier will be free of all responsibility; for example, under the national law at the port of discharge, he may be required to exercise reasonable care of the goods as a bailee.

Thirdly, delivery is effected by the carrier handing over the goods to an authority or other third party to whom, pursuant to local law or regulations at the port of discharge, the goods must be handed over.

Article 5. Basis of Liability

1. The carrier is liable for loss resulting from loss of or damage to the goods, as well as from delay in delivery, if the occurrence which caused the loss, damage or delay took place while the goods were in his charge as defined in Article 4, unless the carrier proves that he, his servants or agents took all measures that could reasonably be required to avoid the occurrence and its consequences.

2. Delay in delivery occurs when the goods have not been delivered at the port of discharge provided for in the contract of carriage by sea within the time expressly agreed upon or, in the absence of such agreement, within the time which it would be reasonable to require of a diligent carrier, having regard to the circumstances of the case.

3. The person entitled to make a claim for the loss of goods may treat the goods as lost if they have not been delivered as required by Article 4 within 60 consecutive days following the expiry of the time for delivery according to paragraph 2 of this Article.

4(a) The carrier is liable:

(i) for loss or damage caused by fire, if the claimant proves that the fire arose from fault or neglect on the part of the carrier, his servants or agents;

(ii) for such loss, damage or delay in delivery which is proved by the claimant to have resulted from the fault or neglect of the carrier, his servants or agents, in taking all measures that could reasonably be required to put out the fire and avoid or mitigate its consequences.

(b) In case of fire on board the ship affecting the goods, if the claimant or the carrier so desires, a survey in accordance with shipping practices must be held into the cause and circumstances of the fire, and a copy of the surveyor's report shall be made available on demand to the carrier and the claimant.

5. With respect to live animals, the carrier is not liable for loss, damage or delay in delivery resulting from any special risk inherent in that kind of carriage. If the carrier proves that he has complied with any special instructions given to him by the shipper respecting the animals and that, in the circumstances of the case, the loss, damage or delay in delivery could be attributed to such risks, it is presumed that the loss, damage or delay in delivery was so caused, unless there is proof that all or a part of the loss, damage or delay in delivery resulted from default or neglect on the part of the carrier, his servants or agents.

6. The carrier is not liable, except in general average, where loss, damage or delay in delivery resulted from measures to save life or from reasonable measures to save property at sea.

7. Where fault or neglect on the part of the carrier, his servants or agents combines with another cause to produce loss, damage or delay in delivery the carrier is liable only to the extent that the loss, damage or delay in delivery is attributable to such fault or neglect, provided that the carrier proves the amount of the loss, damage or delay in delivery not attributable thereto.

Article 5

Article 5 sets out the basis of the carrier's liability for loss, damage and delay to the goods. Liability is based on the principle that the carrier is to be responsible for loss and damage that results from his own fault or neglect, or that of his servants or agents.

Article 5.1 comprises an affirmative statement of responsibility based on a presumption of fault on the part of the carrier for loss or damage to the goods or for delay in delivery while they are in his charge as defined in Article 4.

The philosophy underlying this is set out in clear and concise terms at the end of the Convention, in Annex II. Annex II comprises the Common Understanding of the Parties to the Convention. It states, "the liability of the carrier under this Convention is based on the principle of presumed fault or neglect. This means that, as a rule, the burden of proof rests on the carrier but, with respect to certain cases, the provisions of the Convention modify this rule". Thus, loss or damage suffered by a cargo owner will usually trigger carrier liability unless he can prove a defence under the Convention.

If the carrier is to repudiate liability successfully, he must discharge the burden of proving that he, his servants or agents took all measures that could reasonably be required to avoid not only the occurrence but also its consequences. The most obvious consequence of the new regime for the carrier is the apparent abolition of the obligation to exercise "due diligence" to provide a "seaworthy" ship "before and at the beginning of the voyage", the fulfilment of which enabled him to seek the protection of the exemptions listed in Article IV, Rule 2 of the Hague/Hague-Visby Rules. Although these concepts do not appear in the Hamburg Rules, the real effect of the new régime is to retain the obligation albeit to a much more rigorous extent. Thus, to avoid liability the carrier will need to satisfy the burden of showing that he exercised due diligence to provide a seaworthy ship not merely at the beginning of the voyage but throughout the period of carriage. If relevant to the claim, the carrier must also demonstrate that his servants or agents also took all reasonable measures to avoid the occurrence and its consequences.

This latter requirement removes completely the exception based on: "Act, neglect, or default of the master, mariner, pilot, or the servants of the carrier in the navigation or in the management of the ship".[16] Henceforth the carrier will now be liable for any loss, damage or delay caused by the negligence of the master or crew of the vessel.[17] Under English law the burden of proof under the Hague/Hague-Visby Rules was recently restated by the Admiralty Judge, Mr Justice Clarke.[18] In that case the vessel's shell plating gave way in heavy seas and cargo was lost. Evidence based upon the condition of the vessel's sister ships led the court to conclude that there was a failure to maintain the vessel and to create a proper system for reporting faults.[19] Thus, it is clear that "due diligence" is a wide-ranging obligation which encompasses not only responsibility for the physical state of the vessel at the commencement of the voyage and its manning, but also management and superintendence systems that will ensure that the vessel's condition is fully reported. It may be assumed that the obligation upon a carrier under the Hamburg Rules, to take reasonable precautions would be similarly extensive.

The Convention does not specify how independent contractors are to be dealt with. It therefore remains uncertain whether the new rule will displace the liability

16. Article IV Rule 2(a) of the Hague/Hague-Visby Rules.
17. Subject to the applicability of Article 5.7.
18. *The Toledo* [1995] 1 Lloyd's Rep. 40.
19. But see *The Hellenic Dolphin* [1978] 2 Lloyd's Rep. 336, *The Torenia* [1983] 2 Lloyd's Rep. 210, *The Subro Valour* (1995) LMLN 397.

hitherto imposed upon the carrier for damage caused by the negligence of an independent contractor engaged by him.[20]

Article 5.1 also imposes a liability for delay for which the carrier is responsible unless he can discharge the burden of proving that neither he nor his servants or agents were at fault. This brings the Convention into line with the carriage conventions of CMR, CIM and the Warsaw Convention[21], all of which also make specific provision for loss caused by delay. This is, however, in stark contrast to the position under the Hague/Hague-Visby Rules which do not specifically define delay as a class of recoverable damage. An automatic right to recover for loss caused by delay is therefore created.

In Article 5.2 delay is defined as occurring when the goods have not been delivered at the contractual port of discharge within the time agreed upon between the shipper and the carrier. If there is no agreement the Convention requires delivery to be made within a reasonable time. To determine what is a "reasonable time" the Convention lays down a test that is both objective and subjective. Objective in that the time for delivery is judged by reference to what would be "reasonable to require of a diligent carrier"; subjective, in that the court should have "regard to the circumstances of the case". In a Convention intended to promote uniformity, this is unwelcome.

In Article 5.4 loss, damage or delay in delivery caused by fire is given a self-contained code in which the presumption of fault rule is reversed in favour of the carrier.

Article 5.4. provides therefore that the carrier is only liable for loss, damage or delay caused by fire if the cargo claimant proves either:

1. The fire arose from the fault or neglect on the part of the carrier, his servants or agents; or
2. The carrier, his servants or agents were guilty of fault or neglect in taking all measures that could reasonably be required to put out the fire and avoid or mitigate its consequences.

Article 5.4 represents a frustrating departure from the language of Article 5.1. Normally the carrier must prove that reasonable precautions had been taken to avoid the damage or its consequences. In Article 5.4 it is clear that the burden of proof rests upon the claimant who suffers loss as a result of fire damage. The claimant is not asked to prove that the carrier failed to take reasonable precautions to avoid the fire or loss. Instead the claimant must demonstrate that the fire was caused by "the fault of neglect" of the carrier or crew. It is open to doubt whether "fault or neglect" imposes a different standard of care upon a carrier than the taking of "reasonable precautions". It is submitted that this ought not to be the case but the use of deliberately different language in Article 5.4 is suggestive of a real distinction.

20. *The Muncaster Castle* [1961] AC 807.

21. CIM, International Convention concerning the Carriage of Goods by Rail (CIM) (Bern, 7 February 1970) CMR, Convention on the Contract for the International Carriage of Goods by Road (CMR) (Geneva, 19 May 1956) Warsaw Convention, Convention for the Unification of Certain Rules relating to International Carriage by Air (Warsaw, 12 October 1929).

It remains to be seen, therefore, whether the test laid down in Article 5.1 of "all measures that can reasonably be required to avoid the occurrence and its consequences" is going to be interpreted differently to the test of "fault or neglect" found in Article 5.4 and also Articles 5.5 (Live Animals) and 5.7 (Causation and Damage).

Article 5.4(b) enables either party to commission a survey to establish the cause and circumstances of the fire if it took place on board the ship. On completion of the survey, the report is to be made available to both the carrier and the cargo claimant. The Convention does not say what weight is to be attached to the report.

By Article 5.5 the carriage of live animals is included within the framework of the Hamburg Rules, albeit to a limited extent. The carrier is exempted from liability for any loss, damage or delay in delivery "resulting from any special risks inherent in that kind of carriage". This sentence could be less ambiguous but it is submitted that special risks will be considered in relation both to the type of animal carried and risks generally inherent in the sea transportation of live animals.

Where instructions for the carriage of live animals have been given by the shipper, the carrier can discharge the onus of proof by demonstrating that he complied with those instructions. The carrier remains liable, however, if it is proved that all or articles of the loss, damage or delay resulted from his fault or negligence or that of his servants or agents.

Article 5.6 of the Hamburg Rules distinguishes between measures to save life and measures to save property. In the former, the carrier is exempted from liability for loss, damage or delay which results therefrom. In the latter, the measures taken must be reasonable if the carrier is to be exonerated. Article 5.6 also makes it clear that any general average consequences remain unaffected. The Hamburg Rules do not contain any specific provision concerning deviation, save as is implicit in Article 5.6. Accordingly, the carrier will be liable for loss resulting from deviation unless he can establish the Article 5.1 exemption by demonstrating that he or his servants took "all measures that could reasonably be required to avoid the occurrence and its circumstances". This is obviously a matter of considerable importance. The consequences of unauthorised deviation under English common law were serious (and mitigated only to a limited degree by Article IV, Rule 4 of the Hague/Hague-Visby Rules). A deviating carrier would be treated as acting extra-contractually and would not be entitled to rely upon any of the defences available under the bill of lading whether expressed on the reverse or incorporated as a matter of law, e.g. those set out in Article IV, Rule 2 of the Hague/Hague-Visby Rules. Limits of liability would be treated in the same way. Thus a deviating carrier might find himself subject to unlimited liability even where the deviation was entirely unconnected to the loss complained of.[22] Under the Hamburg Rules a carrier who deviates from the contract will only be liable where loss is caused by such deviation. In most cases damage caused by deviation will be delay (although where perishable goods are concerned it may be more serious). In this situation

22. See e.g. *The Antares (No. 2)* [1987] 1 Lloyd's Rep. 424, and *The Chanda* [1989] 2 Lloyd's Rep. 494, and *The Pembroke* (1994) LMLN 370, NZ High Court.

under the Hamburg Rules, the duty of the carrier is to demonstrate that reasonable precautions were taken to avoid the delay/deviation and costs arising. The carrier will not be deprived of his right to limit liability under Article 6 even where there is an unauthorised deviation. The position of the carrier under the Hamburg Rules is therefore considerably improved over the position under the Hague/Hague-Visby Rules, as under the latter incidental deviation might deprive him of his defences and limits of liability. Under the Hamburg Rules deviation must be causal and the carrier can still escape liability under Article 5.1 or limit it under Article 6. Further, Article 5.6 expressly excludes liability where the carrier acts to save life or takes reasonable steps to save property. This express exclusion is less generous than Article IV Rule 4 of the Hague/Hague-Visby Rules which gives a carrier a blanket protection from the consequences of deviation where he acts to save life or property, i.e. the carrier need not show that deviation undertaken to save property is reasonable.

Article 5.7 is an example of poor draughtsmanship which, in view of the article's potential importance, is regrettable. Its purpose is to enable the carrier to bear responsibility in proportion to fault in circumstances where a third party's negligence has contributed to the loss, damage or delay; provided the carrier can prove "the amount of the loss, damage or delay not attributable thereto". This unfortunate phrasing makes it unclear whether the carrier has to prove merely the degree of fault giving rise to the damage or, as appears likely, the degree of damage to the goods attributable to the negligence of the third party. Given that Article 5.1 makes the carrier responsible for the negligent navigation of the carrying vessel, the significance of this article in collision cases is readily apparent.

However, whilst proving the degree of blame attaching to the colliding vessel may be determined with relative ease, the obligation of showing the proportion of damage attributable thereto may be very much more difficult.

Article 6. Limits of liability

1. (a) The liability of the carrier for loss resulting from loss of or damage to goods according to the provisions of Article 5 is limited to an amount equivalent to 835 units of account per package or other shipping unit or 2.5 units of account per kilogram of gross weight of the goods lost or damaged, whichever is the higher.
   (b) The liability for the carrier for delay in delivery according to the provisions of Article 5 is limited to an amount equivalent to two and a half times the freight payable for the goods delayed, but not exceeding the total freight payable under the contract of carriage of goods by sea.
   (c) In no case shall the aggregate liability of the carrier, under both subparagraphs (a) and (b) of this paragraph, exceed the limitation which would be established under subparagraph (a) of this paragraph for total loss of the goods with respect to which such liability was incurred.

2. For the purpose of calculating which amount is the higher in accordance with paragraph 1(a) of this article, the following rules apply:
   (a) Where a container, pallet or similar article of transport is used to consolidate goods, the package or other shipping units enumerated in the bill of Lading, if issued, or otherwise in any other document evidencing the contract of carriage by sea, as packed in such article of transport are deemed packages or shipping units. Except as aforesaid the goods in such article of transport are deemed one shipping unit

(b) In cases where the article of transport itself has been lost or damaged, that article of transport, if not owned or otherwise supplied by the carrier, is considered one separate shipping unit.

3. Unit of account means the unit of account mentioned in Article 26.

4. By agreement between the carrier and the shipper, limits of liability exceeding those provided for in paragraph 1 may be fixed.

Article 6.1

Article 6.1(a) sets out the limits of liability of the carrier for loss or damage to the goods. The limit of liability for delay in delivery is dealt with in Article 6.1(b).

There are two bases for calculating the limit of liability for loss or damage and the claimant is entitled to the higher figure.

The first method is a calculation based on the package or other shipping unit; here the maximum liability is an amount equal to 835 "units of account" per package or other shipping unit.

The second method is based on the gross weight of the goods lost or damaged; here the maximum liability is an amount equal to 2.5 "units of account" per kilogram of the gross weight of the goods. Article 26 stipulates that the "unit of account" is the Special Drawing Right (SDR). It is applied to the number of packages and the gross weight of the goods included in the bill of lading. A "shipping unit" is not defined but should include the cargo unit itself, e.g. pallet, barrel, package in a container etc. The reference in the Hamburg Rules to "package or shipping unit" is similar to the reference in Article IV, Rule 5 of the Hague/Hague-Visby Rules to "package or unit". Thus, the case law which has accumulated in many common law countries and which seeks to define what is meant by a "package" or "unit" will remain relevant.[23] The limits under the Hague-Visby Rules, as amended, of 2 SDRs and 666.67 SDRs respectively are increased by 25 per cent by the Hamburg Rules.

Article 6.1(b)

The limitation of liability of the carrier for delay has a separate code. Limitation is based on an amount equal to 2.5 times the freight payable for the goods delayed, but not exceeding the total freight payable under the contract of carriage. Accordingly, if cargo representing more than 40 per cent of the total freight for a voyage is delayed the carrier will automatically limit his liability to the total freight payable for that voyage.

Article 6.1 (c)

The total liability of the carrier under all heads cannot exceed the maximum limit on a total loss of the goods as calculated under Article 6.1(a).

23. *Encyclopaedia Britannica Inc.* v. "*Hong Kong Producer*" [1969] 2 Lloyd's Rep. 536, and *The Vermillion Bay* (1990) LMLN 277, *The Tana* (1992) LMLN 323, and *The Hanjin Yosu* (1994) LMLN 371.

Article 6.2

The package limitation rules as they apply to "shipping units" may be summarised thus:

(a) Where the bill of lading enumerates the contents of the container or pallet, each package or other shipping unit is one shipping unit:

e.g. 1 container containing 106 packages = 106 shipping units.[24]

(b) Where the bill of lading does not enumerate the contents of the container or pallet, the container or pallet is one shipping unit:

e.g. 1 container containing general cargo = 1 shipping unit.[25]

(c) Where the bill of lading enumerates the contents of the container or pallet in general terms:

e.g. 1 container containing 7 items of general cargo = 7 shipping units.

(d) Where the bill of lading enumerates the contents of the container as partly packages and partly general cargo, each of the packages is one shipping unit and the general cargo is one shipping unit:

e.g. 1 container containing 7 packages and some general cargo = 8 shipping units.

Article 6.2(a) deals with the situation where the bill of lading does not itself enumerate the contents of the container but there is another document that does and which also evidences the contract of carriage by sea, an example might be the shipping or booking note. In such a case the "other document" may be relied upon in place of the bill of lading to determine the package limitation.

Article 6.2(b) deals with those situations where the claim includes loss or damage to the transport unit itself, most usually a container. In such a case the article of transport is an additional shipping unit if it is not owned or otherwise supplied by the carrier. The article of transport will be "otherwise supplied" if it is delivered to the shipper by someone employed by the carrier, for example the actual carrier.

It is common, where there is container groupage, for the carrier to accept a container stuffed by the forwarding agent (who then becomes the shipper), and to accept an accompanying declaration as to its contents. The bill of lading will then customarily state that the container is "said to contain" a number of packages. Such a statement will not create an estoppel as between the carrier and the shipper nor as between the carrier and a third party to whom the bill of lading has been transferred if the requirements of Article 16 have been complied with by the carrier.

Article 6.4 enables the shipper and the carrier to agree higher levels of limitation than those provided by Article 6.1. Article 15 further provides that such an agreement

24. *The Tana* (1992) under the US Carriage of Goods by Sea Act 1936, and *The Vermillion Bay*, *supra*.

25. Of course, if a significant amount of cargo is lost or damaged the weight-based measure of limitation will apply and the carrier will not be able to limit to 833 SDR for a fully stuffed container.

must be recorded in the bill of lading, although the effect of a failure to comply with Article 15 is unclear. It is submitted that such an omission will not nullify the agreement between the shipper and the carrier. However, it is difficult to envisage the consignee being able to take advantage of such an informal agreement between the shipper and the carrier. The position of the actual carrier is dealt with in Article 10.3.

Article 7. Application to non-contractual claims

1. The defences and limits of liability provided for in this Convention apply in any action against the carrier in respect of loss or damage to the goods covered by the contract of carriage by sea, as well as of delay in delivery whether the action is founded in contract, in tort or otherwise.

2. If such an action is brought against a servant or agent of the carrier, such servant or agent, if he proves that he acted within the scope of his employment, is entitled to avail himself of the defences and limits of liability which the carrier is entitled to invoke under this Convention.

3. Except as provided in Article 8, the aggregate of the amounts recoverable from the carrier and from any persons referred to in paragraph 2 of this Article shall not exceed the limits of liability provided for in this Convention.

Article 7.1

This Rule follows the established regime of the Hague-Visby Rules and ensures that the claimant is not placed in a better position by suing the carrier, actual carrier or their respective servants or agents in tort rather than in contract. The words "or otherwise" would cover an action in bailment.[26]

Article 7.2

This Rule again follows the Hague-Visby regime and extends to the servants and agents of the carrier those defences and limits of liability that are available to the carrier. However, there are three important restrictions. First, the servant or agent must have acted "within the scope of his employment" when the loss or damage occurred. Secondly, the servant or agent must prove this. Thirdly, unlike the Hague-Visby Rules, which specifically excluded them, no mention is made of independent contractors in the Hamburg Rules.

The protection of the Convention is extended to actions against the servants or agents of the actual carrier by virtue of Article 10.2. This has a similar effect to the familiar "Himalaya clause" which is recognised under English law.[27]

26. Hague-Visby Rules Article IV *bis* deals with the problems encountered in *J. Gadsden Pty Ltd and another* v. *Australian Coastal Shipping Commission*. CA [1977] 1 NSWLR 29.07.1977.

27. *The Eurymedon* [1974] 1 Lloyd's Rep. 534. For the position post discharge, see *The Antwerpen* [1994] 1 Lloyd's Rep. 213, New South Wales Court of Appeal

Article 7.3

To avoid the possibility of multiple recoveries, Article 7.3 states that the aggregate of the amounts recoverable from the carrier and his servants or agents shall not exceed the limits provided for in the Convention. This Rule is subject to the provisions of Article 8 which deal with the circumstances in which the right to limit liability is lost.

Article 8. Loss of right to limit responsibility

1. The carrier is not entitled to the benefit of the limitation of liability provided for in Article 6 if it is proved that the loss, damage or delay in delivery resulted from an act or omission of the carrier done with the intent to cause such loss, damage or delay, or recklessly and with knowledge that such loss, damage or delay would probably result.

2. Notwithstanding the provisions of paragraph 2 of Article 7, a servant or agent of the carrier is not entitled to the benefit of the limitation of liability provided for in Article 6 if it is proved that the loss, damage or delay in delivery resulted from an act or omission of such servant or agent, done with the intent to cause such loss, damage or delay, or recklessly and with the knowledge that such loss, damage or delay would probably result.

Article 8.1

This article governs the circumstances in which the carrier will lose the right to limit liability. Similar provisions are found in other transport conventions as follows:

Article 25 of the Warsaw Convention 1929 as amended by Article 13 of the Hague Protocol 1955 provides:

"The limits of liability specified in Article 22 shall not apply if it is proved that the damage resulted from an act or omission of the carrier, his servants or agents done with intent to cause damage or recklessly and with knowledge that damage would probably result; provided that, in the case of such act or omission of a servant or agent, it is also proved that he was acting within the scope of his employment."

Article IV Rule 5 (e) of the Hague-Visby Protocol 1968 provides:

"Neither the carrier nor the ship shall be entitled to the benefit of the limitation of liability provided for in this paragraph if it is proved that the damage resulted from an act or omission of the carrier done with intent to cause damage or recklessly and with knowledge that damage would probably result."

Article 13 of the 1974 Convention on the Carriage of Passengers and their Luggage by Sea provides:

"1. The carrier shall not be entitled to the benefit of the limits of liability prescribed in Article 7 and 8 and paragraph 1 of Article 10, if it is proved that the damage resulted from an act or omission of the carrier done with the intent to cause such damage, or recklessly and with the knowledge that such damage would probably result.

2. The servant or agent of the carrier or of the performing carrier shall not be entitled to the benefit of those limits if it is proved that the damage resulted from an act or omission of that servant or agent done with the intent to cause such damage, or recklessly and with the knowledge that such damage would probably result."

Article 4 of the 1976 Convention on the Limitation of Liability for Maritime Claims provides:

"A person liable shall not be entitled to limit his liability if it is proved that the loss resulted from his personal act or omission committed with the intent to cause such loss, or recklessly and with knowledge that such loss would probably result."

The words of the Hamburg Rules may be considered thus:

"*The carrier is not entitled*." By virtue of Article 10 the actual carrier will be subject to the same regime.

"*If it is proved*." These words make it clear that the burden of proof of challenging the carrier's right to limit liability rests with the claimant.

"*An act or omission of the carrier*." In this context "the carrier" means the carrier himself since his servants or agents are dealt with in Article 8.2.

"*Done with the intent to cause such loss*." The use of these words make it clear that the claimant must prove first, that the carrier had the subjective intent to cause the loss; and secondly that the loss actually suffered is the same as that subjectively intended.

It has been decided[28] under Article IV Rule 5(e) of the Hague-Visby Rules that "intention or recklessness" refers to the state of mind of the owners and does not apply to the reckless acts or omissions of servants or agents of the carrier. Thus the acts of a rogue master or crew are excluded. The distinction between owners and managers is, however, less well respected by the English courts.[29] It may therefore not be safe to automatically assume that an identity of interest between owners and managers will not be found to exist in relation to duties under the Hamburg Rules.

"*Recklessly and with knowledge that such loss ...would probably result*." "Recklessly" in the context of the Warsaw Convention was considered by the Court of Appeal in England in 1983.[30] Eveleigh L.J. stated[31]:

"An act may be reckless when it involves a risk, even though it cannot be said that the danger envisaged is a probable consequence. It is enough that it is a possible consequence, although of course there comes a point where the risk is so remote that it would not be considered reckless to take it. We look for an element of rashness which is perhaps more clearly indicated in the French text "témérairement". Article 25 however refers not to possibility, but to the probability of resulting damage. Thus something more than a possibility is required. The word 'probable' is a common enough word. I understand that to mean that something is likely to happen. I think that is what is meant in Article 25. In other words, one anticipates damage from the act or omission."

28. *The European Enterprise* [1989] 2 Lloyd's Rep. 185.

29. *The Marion* [1984] AC 563, and *The Ert Stefanie* [1989] 1 Lloyd's Rep. 349. It was decided in the latter case that a director of the company managing the vessel was responsible for maintenance and his personal fault in failing to ensure that the vessel was properly maintained was attributable to the owners. Both cases, however, concern liability under the 1957 Limitation Convention where a carrier loses the right to limit liability where loss is caused as a consequence of the "actual fault or privity" of the carrier.

30. *Goldman* v. *Thai Airways International Ltd*. [1983] 3 All ER 693.

31. *Goldman* v. *Thai Airways* has recently been followed by *Gurtner* v. *Beaton* [1993] 2 Lloyd's Rep. 369 and *Antwerp United Diamonds* v. *Air Europe* [1993] 2 Lloyd's Rep. 413. Both cases demonstrate how difficult it will be to break limits of liability. The latter case is important as it demonstrates that an agreement pursuant to Article 6.4 of the Hamburg Rules fixing higher limits than apply under Article 6.1 may not be relied upon by a carrier who causes loss intentionally or recklessly.

Accordingly, the claimant must prove actual (not imputed or constructive) knowledge that the loss suffered by the claimant would probably result from the act or omission in question. It would seem to follow that if the carrier acted with an unreasonable ignorance of the risk of loss, he will not be deprived of the right to limit liability.

Article 8.2

This article makes the servant or agent of the carrier subject to the same rules as the carrier in determining whether they can limit their personal liability. However, no mention is made in Article 8 as to the carrier's liability for the intentional or reckless acts of his servants or agents and presumably this will be left to the national courts to ascertain.

Article 9. Deck cargo

1. The carrier is entitled to carry the goods on deck only if such carriage is in accordance with an agreement with the shipper or with the usage of the particular trade or is required by statutory rules or regulations.

2. If the carrier and the shipper have agreed that the goods shall or may be carried on deck, the carrier must insert in the bill of lading or other document evidencing the contract of carriage by sea a statement to that effect. In the absence of such a statement the carrier has the burden of proving that an agreement for carriage on deck has been entered into; however, the carrier is not entitled to invoke such an agreement against a third party, including a consignee , who has acquired the bill of lading in good faith.

3. Where the goods have been carried on deck contrary to the provision of paragraph 1 of this article or where the carrier may not under paragraph 2 of this article invoke an agreement for carriage on deck, the carrier, notwithstanding the provisions of paragraph 1 of Article 5, is liable for loss of or damage to the goods, as well as for delay in delivery, resulting solely from the carriage on deck, and the extent of his liability is to be determined in accordance with the provisions of Article 6 or Article 8 of this Convention, as the case may be.

4. Carriage of goods on deck contrary to express agreement for carriage under deck is deemed to be an act or omission of the carrier within the meaning of Article 8.

Article 9.1

There are three circumstances in which the carrier is entitled to carry goods on deck.

First, if the carrier has an agreement to do so with the shipper. "Agreement" for this purpose probably does not require an "express agreement", the term used only in Article 9.4 for another purpose. Thus, a liberty clause in the bill of lading on its own should amount to an "agreement" under this article. Support for this view comes from the words "in the bill of lading" which are used in the article rather than "on the face of the bill of lading". Furthermore, Article 15.1(m) also lends weight to this interpretation since it stipulates that the bill of lading should, if applicable, contain a statement "that the goods shall or may be carried on deck".

This provision is less strict than its equivalent of the Hague-Visby Rules. It has been held that, "a mere general liberty to carry goods on deck is not in my view a statement in the contract of carriage that the goods are in fact being carried on deck. To hold otherwise would in my view do violence to the ordinary meaning of the words of Article 1(c) of the [Carriage of Goods By Sea Act, 1924]".[32] In the US it has been decided that stowage of containers on deck can be an unreasonable deviation.[33]

Secondly, deck carriage is permitted if it accords with the "usage of the particular trade". It is submitted that specialised vessels which commonly carry deck cargo, for example container or logger vessels, will satisfy this requirement. However, it is less clear whether a non-specialised vessel, for example a general cargo vessel that carries a container on deck , would meet this requirement.

It is, of course, not sufficient for the carrier to claim that he always stows goods on deck and that the shipper knew about this. This may however prevent (*estop*) the shipper successfully claiming. Such estoppel arise independently of the rules and would not be effective against an ignorant third party, e.g. a consignee.

The third category of permissible deck carriage is where there are statutory or regulatory requirements. This, no doubt, envisages compulsory deck carriage for hazardous or dangerous goods.

Article 9.2.

If a liberty clause is not sufficient to comply with Article 9.1, the carrier has the burden of proving the agreement between himself and the shipper. Where the bill of lading does not mention the agreement, the carrier cannot rely on his agreement with the shipper when the bill of lading has been transferred to a third party who has acquired the bill of lading in good faith. It might nonetheless be possible for a carrier to rely upon a consignee's knowledge of such an agreement independent of the Bill as a defence, relying on an estoppel.

Articles 9.3 and 9.4

When goods have been carried on deck in breach of the three circumstances stated in Article 9.1 or where a third party has acquired the bill of lading in good faith in ignorance of an agreement between the shipper and the carrier permitting deck carriage, then the carrier becomes subject to the regime of liability set forth in Article 5.1.

The sanction for carrying cargo on deck in breach of Articles 9.1 and 9.2 is that the carrier becomes strictly liable for loss, damage or delay resulting solely from the carriage on deck. Illegitimate deck carriage is, however, not akin to deviation as was the case under the Hague/Hague-Visby regime. Under the Hamburg Rules

32. *Svenska Traktor Aktiebolaget* v. *Maritime Agencies (Southampton), Ltd* [1953] 2 Lloyd's Rep. 124 per Pilcher J.

33. *Encyclopaedia Britannica Inc* v. *The "Hong Kong Producer" and Universal Marine Corp.* [1969] 2 Lloyd's Rep. 536.

the carrier is denied the opportunity of avoiding liability by demonstrating that he, his servants or agents took all measures that could reasonably be required to avoid the occurrence and its consequences. Nevertheless, the carrier is still entitled to the benefit of the package limitation provisions of Article 6 save that limitation will be denied if:

(a) the goods are carried on deck in breach of an express agreement to carry them under deck; or
(b) the goods are carried on deck contrary to the provisions of Article 9.1(c) and the claimant can prove the requirements of Article 8, namely that the goods were carried on deck "with the intent to cause such loss, damage or delay; or recklessly and with knowledge that such loss would probably result".

An obvious example of the latter would be sea water damage to an unprotected consignment of cotton carried on deck.

It is important to note that the Hamburg Rules do not enable the carrier to exempt himself from liability where goods are legitimately carried on deck. Thus, legitimate deck carriage will be subject to the Convention in the same way as cargo carried below deck.

Article 10. Liability of the carrier and actual carrier

1. Where the performance of the carriage or part thereof has been entrusted to an actual carrier, whether or nor in pursuance of a liberty under the contract of carriage by sea to do so, the carrier nevertheless remains responsible for the entire carriage according to the provisions of this Convention. The carrier is responsible, in relation to the carriage performed by the actual carrier, for the acts and omissions of the actual carrier and of his servants and agents acting within the scope of their employment.

2. All the provisions of this Convention governing the responsibility of the carrier also apply to the responsibility of the actual carrier for the carriage performed by him. The provisions of paragraphs 2 and 3 of Article 7 and of paragraph 2 of Article 8 apply if an action is brought against a servant or agent of the actual carrier.

3. Any special agreement under which the carrier assumes obligations not imposed by this Convention or waives rights conferred by this Convention affects the actual carrier only if agreed to by him expressly and in writing. Whether or not the actual carrier has so agreed, the carrier nevertheless remains bound by the obligations or waivers resulting from such special agreement.

4. Where and to the extent that both the carrier and the actual carrier are liable, their liability is joint and several.

5. The aggregate of the amounts recoverable from the carrier, the actual carrier and their servants and agents shall not exceed the limits of liability provided for in this Convention.

6. Nothing in this article shall prejudice any right of recourse as between the carrier and the actual carrier.

Article 10.1

The principal object of this article is to ensure that the contractual carrier remains fully responsible for the performance of the carriage notwithstanding that the carriage of the goods has been entrusted to an actual carrier.[34] The main consequence of Article 10.1, combined with Article 14.2, is to render invalid a demise clause or identity of carrier clause. This is only likely to have a practical effect where, for example, a time-charterer's bill contains a demise/identity of carrier clause. In other cases it is likely that, under English law at least, the responsible carrier will be the owner or bareboat charterer. If the vessel is on bareboat charter, whether Article 10 makes the owner and bareboat charterer simultaneously liable is an open question. The definition of "actual carrier" in Article 1.2 includes "any person" who actually performs the contract of carriage. By demise chartering his ship it is difficult to envisage that an owner is performing the contract of carriage and the owner should not be liable in such circumstances.

Article 10.2

This article enables the cargo claimant to bring his action against the actual carrier if the goods suffered loss or damage while they were in his charge.

On a literal reading of the words "All the provisions of this Convention governing the responsibility of the carrier are extended to the actual carrier", it would seem that the actual carrier, whilst obviously being subject to the "responsibility" elements of the Convention, does not have conferred upon him those provisions of the Convention which enable the carrier to exclude liability (Article 5) or to limit liability (Article 6). It is submitted, however, that the courts are unlikely to adopt this interpretation.

Article 10.3

This article gives effect to special agreements under which the carrier assumes additional obligations or waives rights conferred upon him by the Convention.

Whilst the carrier will always be bound by the special agreement, the actual carrier will only be bound if:

(1) he has expressly agreed to the additional obligations or waivers; and
(2) the agreement is in writing.

Article 11. Through carriage

1. Notwithstanding the provisions of paragraph 1 of Article 10, where a contract of carriage by sea provides explicitly that a specified part of the carriage covered by the said contract is to be performed by a named person other than the carrier, the contract may also provide that the carrier is not liable for loss, damage or delay in delivery caused by an occurrence which takes place while the goods are in the charge of the actual carrier during such part of the carriage. Nevertheless, any stipulation limiting or excluding such liability is without effect if no judicial proceedings can be instituted against the actual carrier in a court competent under paragraphs 1 or 2 of Article 21. The burden of proving that any loss, damage or delay in delivery has been caused by such an occurrence rests upon the carrier.

34. An exception to this principle is provided by Article 11.

2. The actual carrier is responsible in accordance with the provisions of paragraph 2 of Article 10 for loss, damage or delay in delivery caused by an occurrence which takes place while the goods are in his charge.

Article 11

The heading of Article 11, "through carriage", is not defined in the Convention and is, in fact, inappropriate since the text of the article is actually concerned with the circumstances by which the carrier can "contract out" of otherwise joint liability.

Thus, Article 11.1 provides a departure from the main rule laid down in Article 10 that the carrier is liable for the performance of the entire contract of carriage by sea. The article enables the carrier to exclude his liability for the period during which the goods are in the charge of the actual carrier provided the following requirements are met:

(1) the actual carrier is named in the contract of carriage; and
(2) details are given in the contract of carriage of that Article of the carriage to be undertaken by the actual carrier; and
(3) the cargo claimant can commence proceedings against the actual carrier in one of the places listed in Article 21.2.

Article 11.2 emphasises that the actual carrier is directly responsible for the goods while they are in his charge.

Article 11, therefore, affords a mechanism enabling a charterer to exclude his liability for ocean carriage in much the same way as was achieved by the use of an identity of carrier clause. Thus a charterer should be able to avoid liability for the sea carriage by taking the following steps:

1. Drafting the bill of lading so that the various stages of the carriage are reduced to their component parts, for example clearance at the port of loading, ocean carriage and clearance at the port of discharge.
2. Specifying in the bill of lading:
   (a) the name of the actual carrier;
   (b) that part of the carriage to be performed by the actual carrier (for example the ocean carriage element); and
   (c) including a clause limiting or excluding the charterer's liability for the specified part of the carriage which he proposes to undertake (for example clearance at the port of loading and/or port of discharge).

Provided the cargo claimant can also sue the actual carrier in one of the places listed in Article 21.2, the carrier (charterer) should be able to limit his liability for any loss, damage or delay to that period during which he was in charge of the goods. If there is an issue as to whether the goods were in the charge of the carrier or the actual carrier on the happening of the occurrence giving rise to the loss, the burden of proving the time of the occurrence rests with the carrier and not the actual carrier.

PART III. LIABILITY OF THE SHIPPER

Article 12. General rule

The shipper is not liable for loss sustained by the carrier or the actual carrier, or for damage sustained by the ship, unless such loss or damage was caused by the fault or neglect of the shipper, his servants or agents. Nor is any servant or agent of the shipper liable for such loss or damage unless the loss or damage was caused by fault or neglect on his part.

Article 12

As a general rule the shipper, his servants or agents have a several liability for loss or damage to the extent only arising from his fault or neglect; however, any such liability is unlimited since the scheme of limitation under the convention applies to the carrier only. This is, of course, the same as the position under the Hague/Hague-Visby Rules.[35] The only distinction is the omission from the Hamburg Rules of "acts". "Fault or neglect" triggers liability under the Hamburg Rules as opposed to "acts, fault or neglect" under the Hague and Hague-Visby Rules. It is also the case that the time limits applicable for the commencement of proceedings will have no automatic application in respect of actions by a carrier against a shipper.

Article 13. Special rules on dangerous goods

1. The shipper must mark or label in a suitable manner dangerous goods as dangerous.

2. Where the shipper hands over dangerous goods to the carrier or an actual carrier, as the case may be, the shipper must inform him of the dangerous character of the goods and, if necessary, of the precautions to be taken. If the shipper fails to do so and such carrier or actual carrier does not otherwise have knowledge of their dangerous character:
   (a) the shipper is liable to the carrier and any actual carrier for the loss resulting from the shipment of such goods, and
   (b) the goods may at any time be unloaded, destroyed or rendered innocuous, as the circumstances may require, without payment of compensation.

3. The provisions of paragraph 2 of this article may not be invoked by any person if during the carriage he has taken the goods in his charge with knowledge of their dangerous character.

4. If, in cases where the provisions of paragraph 2, subparagraph (b), of this article do not apply or may not be invoked, dangerous goods become an actual danger to life or property, they may be unloaded, destroyed or rendered innocuous, as the circumstances may require, without payment of compensation except where there is an obligation to contribute in general average or where the carrier is liable in accordance with the provisions of Article 5.

35. Article IV, Rule 3 reads "the shipper shall not be responsible for loss or damage sustained by the carrier or the ship arising or resulting from any cause without the act, fault or neglect of the shipper, his servants or agents".

Article 13.1

THE CONVENTION DOES NOT DEFINE DANGEROUS GOODS

This is a matter of some significance as under the Hague-Visby Rules it has been decided by the English courts that there must be physical damage. This will include damage to other cargo. In a recent case, a cargo of groundnut pellets were loaded together with other cargo. The groundnuts were infested with insects and damaged other cargo aboard. It was held that the infested groundnuts were dangerous in the sense that they were likely to cause loss to other cargo on board.[36]

A recent case concerning the inter-relation of a carrier's duties under Article III of the Hague Rules, and shipper's responsibilities under Article IV, Rule 6 for shipping dangerous cargo may also be relevant to the scheme of liability prescribed by the Hamburg Rules. It was held that, notwithstanding the loading by a shipper of explosive cargo, the failure on the part of the owners of the vessel to ensure that she was seaworthy was causal and therefore the shippers were not liable.[37] It may therefore be the case under the Hamburg Rules that a shipper responsible for loading dangerous goods may be able to escape liability by pointing to the failure of the carrier to take reasonable precautions under Article 5.1 as the real cause of loss (as opposed to shipper's failure under Article 13). There is no reason in principle why the same analysis should not apply to the inter-relation of Article 5 and Article 13 under the Hamburg Rules.

Article 13.2

The shipper has an absolute obligation to inform the carrier of the dangerous character of the goods and "if necessary" of the precautions to be taken. The use of the words "if necessary" may give rise to dispute. The shipper should certainly disclose any special precautions known to him that would not ordinarily be available to the carrier through the IMO Code.[38] The article appears to contemplate that the shipper's duty is to inform the party to whom he hands over the goods, the carrier or actual carrier as the case may be. It would not be sufficient therefore for the shipper to hand over the goods to the actual carrier but inform only the carrier of their dangerous nature. Presumably, however, if the shipper has properly marked the goods, the actual carrier will "otherwise have knowledge of their dangerous character". If the shipper does not give proper notification to the carrier of the dangerous nature of the goods and if the carrier does not "otherwise have knowledge of their dangerous character" the Convention imposes the sanctions set out in Article 13.2(a) and Article 13.2(b).

It may be assumed that the cost incurred by the carrier or actual carrier of taking the steps permitted under Article 13.2(b) to neutralise the hazard would be recoverable from the shipper under Article 13.2(a).

36. *The Giannis NK* [1994] 2 Lloyd's Rep. 171.
37. *The Fiona* [1994] 2 Lloyd's Rep. 506.
38. IMDG: International Maritime Dangerous Goods Codc, IMO London.

Article 13.4

This article deals with the situation where the shipper has complied with his notification obligations to the carrier or actual carrier and the dangerous goods become an actual danger to life or property. Such an event gives rise to a liberty to unload, destroy or make safe the goods without payment of compensation to the owner of the goods although the general average position is preserved.

PART IV. TRANSPORT DOCUMENTS

Article 14. Issue of bill of lading

1. When the carrier or actual carrier takes the goods in his charge, the carrier must, on demand of the shipper, issue to the shipper a bill of lading.
2. The bill of lading may be signed by a person having authority from the carrier. A bill of lading signed by the master of the ship carrying goods is deemed to have been signed on behalf of the carrier.
3. The signature on the bill of lading may be in handwriting, printed in facsimile, perforated, stamped, in symbols, or made by any other mechanical or electronic means, if not inconsistent with the law of the country where the bill of lading is issued.

Article 14.1

The obligation to issue a bill of lading rests upon the carrier and not the actual carrier. Until the goods have been shipped on board the carrying vessel it will be sufficient for the carrier to issue a "received for shipment" bill of lading. Article 15.2 deals with the circumstances in which a "shipped" bill of lading must be issued.

Article 14.2

The combined effect of the second sentence of Article 14.2 and the provisions of Article 10 is to render invalid an identity of carrier clause. Article 14.2 deems the master signing the bill of lading to be the servant of the carrier (even though he may in reality be the servant of the actual carrier) and Article 10 makes the actual carrier jointly and severally liable with the carrier during the period he is in charge of the goods. However, notwithstanding the provisions of Article 10 and Article 14, there are circumstances in which the carrier can exclude his liability altogether thus leaving only the actual carrier responsible to the claimants. These circumstances are dealt with in Article 11.

Article 15. Contents of the bill of lading

1. The bill of lading must include, *inter alia*, the following particulars:
   (a) the general nature of the goods, the leading marks necessary for identification of the goods, an express statement, if applicable, as to the dangerous character of the

goods the number of packages or pieces, and the weight of the goods or their quantity otherwise expressed, all such particulars as furnished by the shipper;

(b) the apparent condition of the goods;

(c) the name and principal place of business of the carrier;

(d) the name of the shipper;

(e) the consignee if named by the shipper;

(f) the port of loading under the contract of carriage by sea and the date on which the goods were taken over by the carrier at the port of loading;

(g) the port of discharge under the contract of carriage by sea;

(h) the number of originals of the bill of lading, if more than one;

(i) the place of issuance of the bill of lading;

(j) the signature of the carrier or a person acting on his behalf;

(k) the freight to the extent payable by the consignee or other indication that freight is payable by him;

(l) the statement referred to in paragraph 3 of Article 23;

(m) the statement, if applicable, that the goods shall or may be carried on deck;

(n) the date or the period of delivery of the goods at the port of discharge if expressly agreed upon between the parties; and

(o) any increased limit or limits of liability where agreed in accordance with paragraph 4 of Article 6.2.

2. After the goods have been loaded on board, the carrier must issue to the shipper, if the shipper so demands, a "shipped" bill of lading which, in addition to the particulars required under paragraph 1 of this article, must state that the goods are on board a named ship or ships, and the date or dates of loading. If the carrier has previously issued to the shipper a bill of lading or other document of title with respect to any such goods, on request of the carrier, the shipper must surrender such document in exchange for a "shipped" bill of lading. The carrier may amend any previously issued document in order to meet the shipper's demand for a "shipped" bill of lading if, as amended, such document includes all the information required to be contained in a "shipped" bill of lading.

3. The absence in the bill of lading of one or more particulars referred to in this article does not affect the legal character of the document as a bill of lading provided that it nevertheless meets the requirements set out in paragraph 7 of Article 1.

Article 15.1

The list of 15 items in Article 15.1 which "must" be included in the bill of lading is, in fact, limited to nine mandatory items, the remaining six – (e), (h), (k), (m), (n) and (o) – being required only in appropriate circumstances. It should be noted that no particulars of the actual carrier need be given in the bill of lading save in circumstances where the carrier intends to exclude his own liability as provided for in Article 11.

Article 15.1(c)

The requirement to state the "principal place of business of the carrier" may cause difficulty where the carrier is a company registered in one jurisdiction but effective control is exercised by a company registered elsewhere. In *The Blue*

Wave[39] similar considerations arose concerning an owning company registered in Monrovia, Liberia, where the vessel was exclusively managed by a company registered in Greece. On the facts, the court found that the place of business of the managing company met the "principal place of business" criterion of the jurisdiction clause in the bill of lading.

One omission from the list of items to be included in the bill of lading is provision for demurrage incurred at the port of loading which is to be paid by the consignee. Article 16.4 makes clear that the failure to incorporate such a provision in the bill gives rise to an estoppel in favour of the consignee.

Article 16. Bills of lading: reservations and evidentiary effect

1. If the bill of lading contains particulars concerning the general nature, leading marks, number of packages or pieces, weight or quantity of the goods which the carrier or other person issuing the bill of lading on his behalf knows or has reasonable grounds to suspect do not accurately represent the goods actually taken over or, where a "shipped" bill of lading is issued, loaded, or if he had no reasonable means of checking such particulars, the carrier or such other person must insert in the bill of lading a reservation specifying these inaccuracies, grounds of suspicion or the absence of reasonable means of checking.

2. If the carrier or other person issuing the bill of lading on his behalf fails to note on the bill of lading the apparent condition of the goods, he is deemed to have noted on the bill of lading that the goods were in apparent good condition.

3. Except for particulars in respect of which and to the extent to which a reservation permitted under paragraph 1 of this article has been entered:

(a) the bill of lading is *prima facie* evidence of the taking over or, where a "shipped" bill of lading is issued, loading, by the carrier of the goods as described in the bill of lading; and

(b) proof to the contrary by the carrier is not admissible if the bill of lading has been transferred to a third party, including a consignee, who in good faith has acted in reliance on the description of the goods therein.

4. A bill of lading which does not, as provided in paragraph 1, subparagraph (k) of Article 15, set forth the freight or otherwise indicate that freight is payable by the consignee or does not set forth demurrage incurred at the port of lading payable by the consignee, is *prima facie* evidence that no freight or such demurrage is payable by him. However, proof to the contrary by the carrier is not admissible when the bill of lading has been transferred to a third article, including a consignee, who in good faith has acted in reliance on the absence in the bill of lading of any such indication.

Article 16.1

The position under the Hague-Visby Rules and the Hamburg Rules should be broadly similar on the evidential value of statements in Bills. It is only under the Hague Rules that a statement in a bill of lading in the hands of a shipper and a consignee will be *prima facie* evidence of the truth of its terms. It has been clearly

39. *The Blue Wave* [1982] 1 Lloyd's Rep. 151.

established that Article III, Rule 3 of the Hague Rules is of very limited value. It does not prevent a carrier from excluding liability by stating that the information is provided by the shipper or any statement that the condition of goods is not a positive assertion that the goods were shipped in sound condition.[40] There is no reason to believe that a statement in a bill of lading issued under the Hamburg Rules will be of greater value than a similar statement comprised in a Bill which is subject to the Hague or Hague-Visby Rules.

The carrier or other person issuing the bill of lading "must" make a reservation "in the bill of lading" in the following cases:

(a) if he knows the bill of lading particulars are inaccurate, he must specify the inaccuracies;
(b) if he has reasonable grounds to suspect the bill of lading particulars are inaccurate, he must record the grounds of his suspicion.
(c) if he had no reasonable means of checking the bill of lading particulars, he must say so.

Article 16.2

This is a new provision. If the carrier fails to record on the bill of lading the apparent condition of the goods he is deemed to have recorded that they were in "apparent good condition".

Article 16.3

Article 16.3 follows substantially the same scheme as the Hague-Visby Rules in dealing with the consequences to the carrier of issuing a bill of lading that does not contain reservations concerning the condition of the goods on shipment. Thus, as between the carrier and the shipper, a clean bill of lading is *prima facie* evidence of the condition of the goods as described therein. Once a bill of lading has been transferred to a third party, the carrier is estopped from denying shipment of the quantity, number, weight or general nature of the goods as described in the bill. In one respect the Hamburg Rules are not as favourable to the consignee as the Hague-Visby Rules. In order for the estoppel to arise, Article 16.3(b) stipulates that the transferee shall have relied on the description of the goods in the bill when accepting the transfer. This requirement will enable the carrier to prove that the condition of the goods on shipment was known to the person taking up the Bill and that, therefore, the reservation in the bill of lading was not relied upon.

40. *Canada and Dominion Sugar Co.* v. *Canadian National (WI) Co.* [1947] AC 46, and *CN Vascongada* v. *Churchill* [1906] 1 KB 416, and *Silver* v. *Ocean SS Co.* [1930] 1 KB 416, and *Tokio Marine* v. *Retla* [1970] 2 Lloyd's Rep. 91, US Court of Appeals, and *Oricon* v. *Intergraan* [1967] 2 Lloyd's Rep. 82, and *The Pan Queen* (1994) LMLN 389 – US Court of Appeals.

Article 17. Guarantees by the shipper

1. The shipper is deemed to have guaranteed to the carrier the accuracy of particulars relating to the general nature of the goods, their marks, number, weight and quantity as furnished by him for insertion in the bill of lading. The shipper must indemnify the carrier against the loss resulting from inaccuracies in such particulars. The shipper remains liable even if the bill of lading has been transferred by him. The right of the carrier to such indemnity in no way limits his liability under the contract of carriage by sea to any person other than the shipper.

2. Any letter of guarantee or agreement by which the shipper undertakes to indemnify the carrier against loss resulting from the issuance of the bill of lading by the carrier, or by a person acting on his behalf, without entering a reservation relating to particulars furnished by the shipper for insertion in the bill of lading, or to the apparent condition of the goods, is void and of no effect as against any third party, including a consignee, to whom the bill of lading has been transferred.

3. Such letter of guarantee or agreement is valid as against the shipper unless the carrier or the person acting on his behalf, by omitting the reservation referred to in paragraph 2 of this article, intends to defraud a third party, including a consignee, who acts in reliance on the description of the goods in the bill of lading. In the latter case, if the reservation omitted relates to particulars furnished by the shipper for insertion in the bill of lading, the carrier has no right of indemnity from the shipper pursuant to paragraph 1 of this article.

4. In the case of intended fraud referred to in paragraph 3 of this article the carrier is liable, without the benefit of the limitation of liability provided for in this Convention, for the loss incurred by a third party, including a consignee, because he has acted in reliance on the description of the goods in the bill of lading.

Article 17

Articles 17.2–17.4 legislate on letters of indemnity which are commonly issued by a shipper in return for a "clean" bill of lading. The key provisions are to be found in Articles 17.3 and 17.4. Article 17.2. merely states a rather obvious fact, namely that a guarantee from a shipper to a carrier has no legal significance *vis à vis* a third party.

Article 17.3 enables the carrier to enforce a letter of indemnity issued by the shipper unless, by omitting a reservation relating to the particulars furnished by the shipper or relating to the apparent condition of the goods, the carrier intended to defraud a third party who took up the bill of lading in reliance on the description of the goods therein. If an intention to defraud is found, and the reservation omitted concerns the shipper's particulars relating to the general nature of the goods, their mark, number, weight or quantity, then the carrier will also lose the guarantee and right of indemnity against the shipper afforded by Article 17.1.

The position here is in sharp contrast to the basic position under English law. The issuing of a clean bill of lading in circumstances where the damaged condition of the goods upon shipment should have been noted on the Bill will constitute an act of fraud on the part of the carrier in connection with the subsequent negotiation of the Bill. Any letter of indemnity issued in such circumstances will be tainted by fraud and therefore unenforceable.[41]

These provisions have therefore given rise to some controversy. They attempt to give partial legitimacy to a very questionable practice. Concern has also been expressed of the circumstances in which the carrier's right to rely upon the letter of indemnity is lost. In most cases the carrier seldom intends to defraud a third party since he is usually responding to a request from the shipper or charterer who needs a clean bill of lading to meet his letter of credit requirements. The effect of this article may be to encourage the use of letters of indemnity and inaccurate bills of lading. It also has the illogical consequence of enabling the shipper to attempt to avoid his letter of indemnity obligations to the carrier, by alleging an intention to defraud, in circumstances where it was the shipper himself who originated the request for the clean bill of lading.

Article 17.4

The consequences for a carrier who has intended to defraud a third party are severe. The right to limit liability under the Convention is lost.

Article 18. Documents other than bills of lading

Where a carrier issues a document other than a bill of lading to evidence the receipt of the goods to be carried, such document is *prima facie* evidence of the conclusion of the contract of carriage by sea and the taking over by the carrier of the goods as therein described.

Article 18

Article 18 is intended to apply to documents other than bills of lading. Whereas the issue of a bill of lading will normally be conclusive as to the conclusion of the contract of carriage, any other shipping document is merely prima facie evidence of such a contract. Arguably, such a document will only be prima facie evidence of the truth of its contents even in the hands of a consignee. A bill is conclusive under Article 16.3. The practical effect is however likely to be small in the light of the very broad definition of "bill of lading" under Article 1.7. It should also be remembered that a shipper is entitled to demand a bill of lading under Article 14.1 as soon as the carrier takes the goods in his charge.

PART V. CLAIMS AND ACTIONS

Article 19. Notice of loss, damage or delay

1. Unless notice of loss or damage, specifying the general nature of such loss or damage, is given in writing by the consignee to the carrier not later than the working day after the day

41. *Brown Jenkinson & Co* v. *Percy Dalton* [1957] 2 All ER 844.

when the goods were handed over to the consignee, such handing over is *prima facie* evidence of the delivery by the carrier of the goods as described in the document of transport or, if no such document has been issued, in good condition.

2. Where the loss or damage is not apparent, the provisions of paragraph 1 of this article apply correspondingly if notice in writing is not given within 15 consecutive days after the day when the goods were handed over to the consignee.

3. If the state of goods at the time they were handed over to the consignee has been the subject of a joint survey or inspection by the parties, notice in writing need not to be given of loss or damage ascertained during such survey or inspection.

4. In the case of any actual or apprehended loss or damage the carrier and the consignee must give all reasonable facilities to each other for inspecting and tallying the goods.

5. No compensation shall be payable for loss resulting from delay in delivery unless a notice has been given in writing to the carrier within 60 consecutive days after the day when the goods were handed over to the consignee.

6. If the goods have been delivered by an actual carrier, any notice given under this article to him shall have the same effect as if it had been given to the carrier, and any notice given to the carrier shall have effect as if given to such actual carrier.

7. Unless notice of loss or damage, specifying the general nature of the loss or damage, is given in writing by the carrier or actual carrier to the shipper not later than 90 consecutive days after the occurrence of such loss or damage or after the delivery of the goods in accordance with paragraph 2 of Article 4, whichever is later, the failure to give such notice is *prima facie* evidence that the carrier or the actual carrier has sustained no loss or damage due to the fault or neglect of the shipper, his servants or agents.

8. For the purpose of this article, notice given to a person acting on the carrier's or the actual carrier's behalf, including the master or the officer in charge of the ship, or to a person acting on the shipper's behalf is deemed to have been given to the carrier, to the actual carrier or to the shipper, respectively.

Articles 19.1, 19.2 and 19.6

Article 19.1 requires the consignee to give written notice of loss or damage not later than the working day after delivery. In cases of latent damage, Article 19.2 requires the notice to be given within 15 consecutive days after the day of delivery. In both cases the failure to give written notice constitutes *prima facie* evidence of delivery in good condition.

The written notice may be given to the carrier, the actual carrier or, by virtue of Article 19.6, to someone acting on their behalf including the master or officer in charge of the ship.

Article 19.5

The time limit for claiming compensation for delay is extended to 60 consecutive days after delivery of the goods. If there is a failure to give such notice, the claim is extinguished. As in the case of damage to the goods, the written notice may be given to the carrier, actual carrier or a person acting on their behalf, including the master or officer in charge of the ship. It is clear from the provisions of Article 19.5 that compensation for delay in delivery does not arise where the goods are never delivered to the consignee, for example where the goods are stolen from the port of discharge prior to delivery. In this eventuality the remedy of the consignee is limited to seeking compensation for loss of the goods.

Article 19.7

The claim by the carrier or actual carrier against the shipper for loss or damage must be given in writing within 90 consecutive days of either:

(1) the occurrence; or

(2) delivery of the goods

A failure so to do constitutes *prima facie* evidence that no loss or damage has been sustained.

Article 20. Limitation of actions

1. Any action relating to carriage of goods under this Convention is time-barred if judicial or arbitral proceedings have not been instituted within a period of two years.

2. The limitation period commences on the day on which the carrier has delivered the goods or part thereof or, in cases where no goods have been delivered, on the last day on which the goods should have been delivered. The day on which the limitation period commences is not included in the period

3. The person against whom a claim is made may at any time during the running of the limitation period extend that period by a declaration in writing to the claimant. This period may be further extended by another declaration or declarations.

4. An action for indemnity by a person held liable may be instituted even after the expiration of the limitation period provided for in the preceding paragraphs if instituted within the time allowed by the law of the State where proceedings are instituted. However, the time allowed shall not be less than 90 days commencing from the days when the person instituting such action for indemnity has settled the claim or has been served with process in the action against himself.

Article 20

Under the Hamburg Rules the provisions concerning limitation of action are straightforward. However, one area which may give rise to difficulty is in the case of non-delivery where the two-year period is calculated from the last day on which the goods should have been delivered. Determining when the goods should have been delivered may give rise to argument given the extended definition of delivery in Article 4.2.

Article 21. Jurisdiction

1. In judicial proceedings relating to carriage of goods under this Convention the plaintiff, at his option, may institute an action in a court which, according to the law of the State where the court is situated, is competent and within the jurisdiction of which is situated one of the following places:

(a) the principal place of business or, in the absence thereof, the habitual residence of the defendant; or

(b) the place where the contract was made provided that the defendant has there a place of business, branch or agency through which the contract was made; or

(c) the port of loading or the port of discharge; or

(d) any additional place designated for that purpose in the contract of carriage by sea.

2. (a) Notwithstanding the preceding provisions of this Article, an action may be instituted in the courts of any port or place in a Contracting State at which the carrying vessel or any other vessel of the same ownership may have been arrested

in accordance with applicable rules of the law of that State and of international law. However, in such a case at the petition of the defendant, the claimant must remove the action, at his choice, to one of the jurisdictions referred to in paragraph 1 of this Article for the determination of the claim, but before such removal the defendant must furnish security sufficient to ensure payment of any judgment that may subsequently be awarded to the claimant in the action.

(b) All questions relating to the sufficiency or otherwise of the security shall be determined by the court of the port or place of the arrest.

3. No judicial proceedings relating to carriage of goods under this Convention may be instituted in a place not specified in paragraphs 1 or 2 of this article. The provisions of this paragraph do not constitute an obstacle to the jurisdiction of the Contracting States for provisional or protective measures.

4. (a) Where an action has been instituted in a court competent under paragraphs 1 or 2 of this article or where judgment has been delivered by such a court, no new action may be started between the same parties on the same grounds unless the judgment of the court before which the first action was instituted is not enforceable in the country in which the new proceedings are instituted;

(b) for the purpose of this article the institution of measures with a view to obtaining enforcement of a judgment is not to be considered as the starting of a new action;

(c) for the purpose of this article, the removal of an action to a different court within the same country, or to a court in another country, in accordance with paragraph 2(a) of this Article, is not to be considered as the starting of a new action.

5. Notwithstanding the provisions of the preceding paragraphs, an agreement made by the parties, after a claim under the contract of carriage by sea has arisen, which designates the place where the claimant may institute an action, is effective.

Article 21

The rules relating to jurisdiction cannot be described as a model of clarity. However, the key feature is that the carrier is prevented from imposing his choice of forum by the use of a jurisdiction clause in the bill of lading. It should be remarked that a carrier did not enjoy an unfettered right under the Hague/Hague-Visby Rules to dictate the jurisdiction in which a cargo claimant might proceed, as illustrated by an Australian case.[42] There, bills of lading issued at Dunkirk for a voyage to Sydney prescribed French law and jurisdiction. Proceedings were commenced in the Australian courts by receivers of the cargo. It was decided by the Australian court that the French jurisdiction clause was unlawful in ousting the jurisdiction of the Australian courts. It breached Article III, Rule 8 of the Hague Rules. The position is the same in a number of European countries.

The focus of Article 21 is jurisdiction. It is not directly concerned with the applicable law which governs the contract of carriage. It is therefore open to a carrier to attempt to prescribe the system of law under which liability is to be determined, even if that law has to be applied by a foreign court. It will of course be a matter for the court in which the claimant elects to sue under Article 21 to decide whether to respect the owners' choice of law. The English courts are likely to be prepared to apply a foreign law in proceedings before them.

42. *Wilson* v. *Cie des Messageries Maritimes* [1954] 2 Lloyd's Rep. 544 (NSW).

Article 21.1 stipulates five places where the claimant ("plaintiff") may, at his option, institute proceedings. However, whether or not such proceedings can actually be commenced in any of the five places will depend upon the national law of each place since the Convention does not itself purport to confer jurisdiction through its own provisions.

By Article 21.2 a sixth place is added to the list of places in which proceedings may be instituted, namely the place at which the ship can be arrested. However, such proceedings must be moved to one of the five principal places of jurisdiction if the defendant so requests and furnishes adequate security for the claim.

Article 21.3 expressly prohibits the commencement of proceedings on the merits in any place other than the six specified in articles 21.1 and 21.2. This restriction does not, however, preclude the taking of conservatory steps in a Contracting State nor does it prevent the parties from agreeing to an alternative jurisdiction after the claim has arisen since this is allowed by Article 21.5.

The rationale behind Article 21.4 is unclear. The article, without making clear why, appears to enable the commencement of duplicate proceedings against the carrier or actual carrier in a jurisdiction other than the court first seized, if a judgment of that court is not recognised by the courts where the duplicate proceedings are commenced.

Article 22. Arbitration

1. Subject to the provisions of this article, parties may provide by agreement evidenced in writing that any dispute that may arise relating to carriage of goods under this Convention shall be referred to arbitration.

2. Where a charterparty contains a provision that disputes arising thereunder shall be referred to arbitration and a bill of lading issued pursuant to the charterparty does not contain a special annotation providing that such provision shall be binding upon the holder of the bill of lading, the carrier may not invoke such provision as against a holder having acquired the bill of lading in good faith.

3. The arbitration proceedings shall, at the option of the claimant, be instituted at one of the following places:

(a) a place in a State within whose territory is situated:

(i) the principal place of business of the defendant or, in the absence thereof, the habitual residence of the defendant; or

(ii) the place where the contract was made, provided that the defendant has there a place of business, branch or agency through which the contract was made; or

(iii) the port of loading or the port of discharge; or

(b) any place designated for that purpose in the arbitration clause or agreement.

4. The arbitrator or arbitration tribunal shall apply the rules of this Convention.

5. The provisions of paragraphs 3 and 4 of this article are deemed to be part of every arbitration clause or agreement, and any term of such clause or agreement which is inconsistent therewith is null and void.

6. Nothing in this article affects the validity of an agreement relating to arbitration made by the parties after the claim under the contract of carriage by sea has arisen.

Article 22.1

This article expressly recognises the validity of arbitration agreements "evidenced in writing". In the simple case of a carrier contracting with a shipper where the bill of lading contains an arbitration clause no particular difficulty arises. It remains unclear, however, whether an "actual carrier" would be bound by such an arbitration clause, particularly as he may have no prior knowledge of its existence. This problem may well be overcome by the principle of ostensible authority under English law, at least where the Bill purports by its terms to be a contract between the "merchant" and the actual carrier. The scheme of the Convention is to make the actual carrier jointly and severally liable with the carrier. Arguably the actual carrier could invoke Article 10.3 in order to avoid the effect of the arbitration agreement. The recognition of arbitration by the Hamburg Rules is an advance on the previous position. Under the Hague Rules a number of jurisdictions declined to recognise arbitration clauses in bills of lading.

There must however be serious doubts as to the practicality of Article 22. As with Article 21 no law is prescribed. It will therefore be open to the carrier to try to impose a choice of law. So far as English law is concerned, it is important to specify a law since arbitration with a "floating" law clause is not permitted. A floating jurisdiction clause is however allowed.[43]

Article 22.2 is a helpful clarification in respect of bills of lading issued pursuant to a charterparty which purportedly incorporate the arbitration clause. Henceforth, in order to be effective against a consignee without notice of the clause, the bill of lading must contain a "special annotation" stipulating that the arbitration clause will be binding.

Article 22.3 adopts the same philosophy as applies to choice of forum clauses under Article 21.

The claimant may choose the venue of the arbitration notwithstanding the terms of the arbitration clause itself. These venues correspond with those listed in Article 21.1 and are as follows:

(a) the place designated in the arbitration clause;
(b) the principal place of business of the defendant or, in the absence thereof, his habitual residence; or
(c) the place where to contract was made, provided that the defendant has there a place of business, branch or agency through which the contract was made; or
(d) the port of loading; or
(e) the port of discharge.

Article 22.5

Article 22.5 regulates all arbitration clauses by deeming the right of the claimant to choose one of the six specified places to be a part of every arbitration agreement

43. *The Star Texas* [1993] 2 Lloyd's Rep. 445.

and making null and void all provisions inconsistent therewith or inconsistent with any provision that seeks to enable the arbitrator to depart from the Hamburg Rules.

Article 22.6

This article enables the parties to submit an existing dispute to arbitration at a venue of their choice.

PART VI. SUPPLEMENTARY PROVISIONS

Article 23. Contractual stipulations

1. Any stipulation in a contract of carriage by sea, in a bill of lading, or in any other document evidencing the contract of carriage by sea is null and void to the extent that it derogates, directly or indirectly, from the provisions of this Convention. The nullity of such a stipulation does not affect the validity of the other provisions of the contract or document of which it forms part. A clause assigning benefit of insurance of the goods in favour of the carrier, or any similar clause, is null and void.

2. Notwithstanding the provisions of paragraph 1 of this article, a carrier may increase his responsibilities and obligations under this Convention.

3. Where a bill of lading or any other document evidencing the contract of carriage by sea is issued, it must contain a statement that the carriage is subject to the provisions of this Convention which nullify any stipulation derogating therefrom to the detriment of shipper or the consignee.

4. Where the claimant in respect of the goods has incurred loss as a result of a stipulation which is null and void by virtue of the present article, or as a result of the omission of the statement referred to in paragraph 3 of this article, the carrier must pay compensation to the extent required in order to give the claimant compensation in accordance with the provisions of this Convention for any loss of or damage to the goods as well as for delay in delivery. The carrier must, in addition, pay compensation for costs incurred by the claimant for the purpose of exercising his right, provided that costs incurred in the action where the foregoing provision is invoked are to be determined in accordance with the law of the State where proceedings are instituted.

Article 23

Article 23.1 makes null and void any clause in a bill of lading or other document evidencing the contract of carriage by sea, to the extent that it derogates "directly or indirectly" from the provisions of the Convention. The censure thus applicable to clauses which indirectly derogate from the Convention is wholly new. This provision seems to be aimed at clauses that offend against the spirit if not the letter of the Convention, which, if correct, may reduce the scope of drafting bills of lading to avoid the full rigours of the Convention.

Article 23.4 is noteworthy if only because of the potential difficulty in its operation. It appears to contemplate that a claimant, who has recovered less than that to which he is entitled under the Convention, may sue the carrier to recoup his loss on the ground that either he was misled by a "null and void" clause or that the bill of lading did not contain a statement giving paramountcy to the Hamburg Rules. A claimant who is misled by a null and void clause into accepting less than his entitlement has, in most cases, made a mistake of law for which there would be no redress against the carrier.

The second limb, which contemplates a loss by reason of the omission of a Hamburg Rules clause paramount, is also likely to raise difficulties.

Article 24. General average

1. Nothing in this Convention shall prevent the application of provisions in the contract of carriage by sea or national law regarding the adjustment of general average.

2. With the exception of Article 20, the provisions of this Convention relating to the liability of the carrier for loss of or damage to the goods also determine whether the consignee may refuse contribution in general average and the liability of the carrier to indemnify the consignee in respect of any such contribution made or salvage paid.

Article 24.1

The Hamburg Rules make no change to the circumstances in which general average may be declared by a carrier as is made clear by Article 24.1. Article 24.2 makes clear that the obligation to contribute in general average will follow the liability regime under the Rules.

Article 25. Other conventions

1. This Convention does not modify the rights or duties of the carrier, the actual carrier and their servants and agents, provided for in international conventions or national law relating to the limitation of liability of owners of seagoing ships.

2. The provisions of Articles 21 and 22 of this Convention do not prevent the application of the mandatory provisions of any other multilateral convention already in force at the date of this Convention relating to matters dealt with in the said articles, provided that the dispute arises exclusively between the parties having their principal place of business in States members of such convention. However, this paragraph does not affect the application of paragraph 4 of Article 22 of this Convention.

3. No liability shall arise under the provisions of this Convention for damage cause by a nuclear incident if the operator of a nuclear installation is liable for such damage:

(a) under either the Paris Convention of 29 July 1960, as amended by the Additional Protocol of 28 January 1964 or the Vienna Convention of 21 May 1963, on Civil Liability for Nuclear Damage; or

(b) by virtue of national law governing the liability for such damage, provided that such law is in all respects as favourable to persons who may suffer damages as either the Paris or Vienna Conventions.

4. No liability shall arise under the provisions of this Convention for any loss of or damage to or delay in delivery of luggage for which the carrier is responsible under any international convention or national law relating to the carriage of passengers and their luggage by sea.

5. Nothing contained in this Convention prevents a Contracting State from applying any other international convention which is already in force at the date of this Convention and

which applies mandatorily to contracts of carriage of goods primarily by a mode of transport other than transport by sea. This provision also applies to any subsequent revision or amendment of such international convention.

Article 25.2

Article 25.2 expressly recognises the mandatory application of other conventions already in force in relation to the jurisdiction provisions of Article 21 and 22. One such convention which may well curtail the ability of the claimant to choose the jurisdiction in which to commence proceedings is the 1968 Brussels Convention on Jurisdiction and the Enforcement of Judgments in Civil and Commercial Matters.[44] Whilst the Brussels Convention will not affect Article 22, since arbitration is expressly excluded from the scope of its operation, the provisions, where applicable, concerning the forum in which judicial proceedings may be commenced will take precedence over Article 21 of the Hamburg Rules.

Overall, the effect of Article 25 is to ensure that the liability regime introduced by the Rules is expressly subject to the 1957 and 1976 Limitation Conventions. With the higher limits of liability recognised by the Hamburg Rules the ability of a carrier to limit his liability by reference to the vessels' tonnage is of greater relevance than was the case under the Hague/Hague-Visby Rules. At present, however, only Egypt is a party to the Hamburg Rules and one of the Limitation Conventions, the 1976 London Convention.

Article 26. Unit of account

1. The unit of account referred to in Article 6 of this Convention is the Special Drawing Right as defined by the International Monetary Fund. The amounts mentioned in Article 6 are to be converted into the national currency of a State according to the value of such currency at the date of judgment or the date agreed upon by the parties. The value of a national currency, in terms of the Special Drawing Right, of a Contracting State which is a member of the International Monetary Fund is to be calculated in accordance with the method of valuation applied by the International Monetary Fund in effect at the date in question for its operations and transactions. The value of a national currency in terms of the Special Drawing Right of a Contracting State which is not a member of the International Monetary Fund is to be calculated in a manner determined by the State.

2. Nevertheless, those States which are not members of the International Monetary Fund and whose law does not permit the application of the provisions of paragraph 1 of the article may, at the time of signature, or at the time of ratification, acceptance, approval or accession or at any time thereafter, declare that the limits of liability provided for in this Convention to be applied in their territories shall be fixed as: 12,500 monetary units per package or other shipping unit or 37.5 monetary units per kilogram of gross weight of the goods.

3. The monetary unit referred to in paragraph 2 of this article corresponds to sixty-five and a half milligrams of gold of millesimal fineness nine hundred. The conversion of the amounts referred to in paragraph 2 into the national currency is to be made according to the law of the State concerned.

4. The calculation mentioned in the last sentence of paragraph 1 and the conversion

44. As will the Lugano Convention of 1987.

mentioned in paragraph 3 of this Article is to be made in such a manner as to express in the national currency of the Contracting State as far as possible the same real value for the amounts in Article 6 as is expressed there in units of account. Contracting States must communicate to the depository the manner of calculation pursuant to paragraph 1 of this article, or the result of the conversion mentioned in paragraph 3 of this article, as the case may be, at the time of signature or when depositing their instruments of ratification, acceptance, approval or accession, or when availing themselves of the option provided for in paragraph 2 of this article and whenever there is a change in the manner of such calculation or in the result of such conversion.

PART VII. FINAL CLAUSES

Article 27. Depository

The Secretary-General of the United Nations is hereby designated as the depository of this Convention.

Article 28. Signature, ratification, acceptance, approval, accession

1. This Convention is open for signature by all States until 30 April 1979, at the Headquarters of the United Nations, New York.
2. This Convention is subject to ratification, acceptance or approval by the signatory States.
3. After 30 April 1979, this Convention will be open for accession by all States which are not signatory States.
4. Instruments of ratification, acceptance, approval and accession are to be deposited with the Secretary-General of the United Nations.

Article 29. Reservations

No reservations may be made to this Convention

Article 30. Entry into force

1. This Convention enters into force on the first day of the month following the expiration of one year from the date of deposit of the twentieth instrument of ratification, acceptance, approval or accession.
2. For each State which becomes a Contracting State to this Convention after the date of the deposit of the twentieth instrument of ratification, acceptance, approval or accession, this Convention enters into force on the first day of the month following the expiration of one year after the deposit of the appropriate instrument on behalf of that State.
3. Each Contracting State shall apply the provisions of this Convention to contracts of carriage by sea concluded on or after the date of entry into force of this Convention in respect of that State.

Article 31. Denunciation of other conventions

1. Upon becoming a Contracting State to this Convention, any State party to the International Convention for the Unification of Certain Rules relating to Bills of Lading signed at Brussels on 25 August 1924 (1924 Convention) must notify the Government of Belgium as the depository of the 1924 Convention of its denunciation of the said Convention with a declaration that the denunciation is to take effect as from the date when this Convention enters into force in respect of that State.

2. Upon the entry into force of this Convention under paragraph 1 of Article 30, the depository of this Convention must notify the Government of Belgium as the depository of the 1924 Convention of the date of such entry into force, and of the names of the Contracting States in respect of which the Convention has entered into force.

3. The provisions of paragraphs 1 and 2 of this article apply correspondingly in respect of States Parties to the Protocol signed on 23 February 1968, to amend the International Convention for the Unification of Certain Rules relating to Bills of Lading signed at Brussels on 25 August 1924.

4. Notwithstanding Article 2 of this Convention, for the purposes of paragraph 1 of this article, a Contracting State may, if it deems it desirable, defer the denunciation of the 1924 Convention and of the 1924 Convention as modified by the 1968 Protocol for a maximum period of five years from the entry into force of this Convention. It will then notify the Government of Belgium of its intention. During this transitory period, it must apply to the Contracting States this Convention to the exclusion of any other one.[45]

Article 32. Revision and amendment

1. At the request of not less than one-third of the Contracting States to this Convention, the depository shall convene a conference of the Contracting States for revising or amending it.

2. Any instrument of ratification, acceptance, approval or accession deposited after the entry into force of an amendment to this Convention, is deemed to apply to the Convention as amended.

Article 33. Revision of the limitation amounts and unit of account or monetary unit

1. Notwithstanding the provisions of Article 32, a conference only for the purpose of altering the amount specified in Article 6 and paragraph 2 of Article 26, or of substituting either or both of the units defined in paragraphs 1 and 3 of Article 26 by other units is to be convened by the depository in accordance with paragraph 2 of this article. An alteration of the amounts shall be made only because of a significant change in their real value.

2. A revision conference is to be convened by the depository when not less than one-fourth of the Contracting States so request.

3. Any decision by the conference must be taken by a two-thirds majority of the participating States. The amendment is communicated by the depository to all the Contracting States for acceptance and to all the States signatories of the Convention for information.

45. Authors footnote: This "afterthought" in respect of a transitory period of five years is one of the late amendments; it was not discussed because of lack of time and was added without the mutual consent of all Conference members having been obtained.

4. Any amendment adopted enters into force on the first day of the month following one year after its acceptance by two-thirds of the Contracting States. Acceptance is to be effected by the deposit of a formal instrument to that effect, with the depository.

5. After entry into force of an amendment a Contracting State which has accepted the amendment is entitled to apply the Convention as amended in its relations with contracting States which have not within six months after the adoption of the amendment notified the depository that they are not bound by the amendment.

6. Any instrument of ratification, acceptance, approval or accession deposited after the entry into force of an amendment to this Convention, is deemed to apply to the Convention as amended.

Article 34. Denunciation

1. Contracting State may denounce this Convention at any time by means of a notification in writing addressed to the depository.

2. The denunciation takes effect on the first day of the month following the expiration of one year after the notification is received by the depository. Where a longer period is specified in the notification, the denunciation takes effect upon the expiration of such longer period after the notification is received by the depository.

DONE at Hamburg, this thirty-first day of March one thousand nine hundred and seventy-eight, in a single original, of which the Arabic, Chinese, English, French, Russian and Spanish texts are equally authentic.

IN WITNESS WHEREOF the undersigned plenipotentiaries, being duly authorised by their respective Governments, have signed the present Convention.

ANNEX II. COMMON UNDERSTANDING

Adopted by The United Nations Conference on the Carriage of Goods by Sea.

It is the common understanding that the liability of the carrier under this Convention is based on the principle of presumed fault or neglect. This means that, as a rule, the burden of proof rests on the carrier but, with respect to certain cases, the provisions of the Convention modify this rule.

ANNEX III. FINAL RESOLUTION

Resolution adopted by the United Nations Conference on the Carriage of Goods by Sea.
The United Nations Conference on the Carriage of Goods by Sea,

Noting with appreciation the kind invitation of the Federal Republic of Germany to hold the Conference in Hamburg,

Being aware that the facilities placed at the disposal of the Conference and the generous hospitality bestowed on the participants by the Government of the Federal Republic of Germany and by the Free and Hanseatic city of Hamburg, have in no small measure contributed to the success of the Conference,

Expresses its gratitude to the Government and people of the Federal Republic of Germany, and Having adopted the Convention on the Carriage of Goods by Sea on the basis of a draft Convention prepared by the United Nations Commission on International Trade Law at the request of the United Nations Conference on Trade and Development,

Expresses its gratitude to the United Nations Commission on International Trade Law and to the United Nations Conference on Trade and Development for their outstanding contribution to the simplification and harmonisation of the law of the carriage of goods by sea, and

Decides to designate the Convention adopted by the Conference as the: "UNITED NATIONS CONVENTION ON THE CARRIAGE OF GOODS BY SEA, 1978" and

Recommends that the rules embodied therein be known as the "HAMBURG RULES".

APPENDIX I

TABLE OF OTHER CONVENTIONS

Arbitral Awards Convention

Convention on the Recognition and Enforcement of Foreign Arbitral Page 186 Awards (New York, 10 June 1958)

Arrest Convention

International Convention for the Unification of Certain Rules relating to the Arrest of Sea-going Ships (Brussels, 10 May 1952)

Athens Convention

Convention relating to the Carriage of Passengers and their Luggage by Sea (Athens, 13 December 1974)

Brussels Convention

International Convention relating to the Limitations of Liability of Owners of Sea-going Ships (Brussels, 10 October 1957)

CIM

International Convention concerning the Carriage of Goods by Rail (CIM) (Bern, 7 February 1970)

CMR

Convention on the Contract for the International Carriage of Goods by Road (CMR) (Geneva, 19 May 1956)

COTIF

Convention concerning International Transport by Rail (COTIF) (Bern, 9 May 1980)

COTIF-Appendix CIM

Uniform Rules concerning the Contract for International Carriage of Goods by Rail (CIM), Appendix B to the Convention concerning International Transport by Rail (COTIF) (Bern, 9 May 1980)

Guadalajara Convention

Convention supplementary to the Warsaw Convention for the Unification of Certain Rules relating to International Carriage by Air performed by a Person other than the Contracting Carrier (Guadalajara, 18 September 1961)

Hague Protocol

Protocol to amend the Warsaw Convention of 12 October 1919 for the Unification of Certain Rules relating to International Carriage by Air (The Hague, 28 September 1955)

Hague Rules

International Convention for the Unification of Certain Rules of Law relating to Bills of Lading (Brussels, 25 August 1924)

London Convention

Convention on Limitation of Liability for Maritime Claims, 1976 (London, 19 November 1976)

MT Convention

United Nations Convention on International Multimodal Transport of Goods (Geneva, 1980)

Vienna Convention

Convention on the Law of Treaties (Vienna, 23 May 1969)

Visby Protocol

Protocol to amend the Brussels International Convention of 25 August 1924 for the Unification of Certain Rules of Law relating to Bills of Lading (23 February 1968)

Warsaw Convention

Convention for the Unification of Certain Rules relating to International Carriage by Air (Warsaw, 12 October 1929)

York-Antwerp Rules 1974

(Hamburg, 4 April 1974)

Brussels Convention

on Jurisdiction and the Enforcement of Judgments in Civil and Commercial Matters 1968.

Lugano Convention

on Jurisdiction and the Enforcement of Judgments in Civil Matters 1987.

APPENDIX 2

THE HAMBURG RULES

SIGNATORIES AND CONTRACTING STATES AS OF 19 FEBRUARY 1995

Ratification/Accession

1. Austria,	29 July 1993
2. Barbados,	2 February 1981
3. Botswana,	16 February 1988
4. Burkina Faso,	14 August 1989
5. Cameroon,	21 October 1994
6. Chile,	9 July 1982[1]
7. Egypt,	23 April 1979[2]
8. Guinea,	23 January 1991
9. Hungary,	5 July 1984
10. Kenya,	31 July 1989[3]
11. Lebanon,	4 April 1983
12. Lesotho,	26 October 1989
13. Malawi,	18 March 1991
14. Morocco,	12 June 1981
15. Nigeria,	7 November 1988[4]
16. Romania,	7 January 1982[5]
17. Senegal,	17 March 1986
18. Sierra Leone,	7 October 1988
19. Tanzania,	24 July 1979
20. Tunisia,	15 September 1980
21. Uganda,	6 July 1979
22. Zambia,	7 October 1991[6]

1. Chile, which ratified the Hamburg Rules on 9 July 1982, recently gave consideration to denouncing them. An inter-departmental committee of the Chilean Government concluded that denunciation would be premature as the Rules had only been in force internationally since 1 November 1992. The committee decided that the matter should be reviewed if it transpired that Chile's adherence to the Hamburg Rules hindered its foreign trade.

2. Egypt deferred denunciation of the Hague-Visby Rules for the maximum allowed of five years and continues to apply the regime in its trade with other than Hamburg Rules countries.

3. Kenya acceded to the Hamburg Rules on 31 July 1989 but is understood not to be applying them.

4. Nigeria acceded to the Hamburg Rules on 7 November 1988 but is understood not to be applying them.

5. Romania acceded to the Hamburg Rules on 7 January 1982 but is understood not to be applying them.

6. Zambia acceded to the Hamburg Rules on 7 October 1991 but is understood not to be applying them.

Contracting States	*Signatures*
Austria,	30 April 1979
Brazil,	31 March 1978
Chile,	31 March 1978
Czechoslovakia,	6 March 1979[7]
Denmark,	18 April 1979
Ecuador,	31 March 1978
Egypt,	31 March 1978
Finland,	18 April 1979
France,	18 April 1979
Germany,	31 March 1978[8]
Ghana,	31 March 1978
Holy See,	31 March 1978
Hungary,	23 April 1979
Madagascar,	31 March 1978
Mexico,	31 March 1978
Norway,	18 April 1979
Pakistan,	8 March 1979
Panama,	31 March 1978
Philippines,	14 June 1978
Portugal,	31 March 1978
Senegal,	31 March 1978
Sierra Leone,	15 August 1978
Singapore,	31 March 1978
Sweden,	18 April 1979
United States of America,	30 April 1979
Venezuela,	31 March 1978
Zaire	19 April 1979

7. Upon signing the Convention the Czechoslovak Socialist Republic declared in accordance with Article 26 a formula for converting the amounts of liability referred to in paragraph 2 of that article into Czechoslovak currency and the amount of the limits of liability to be applied in the territory of the Czechoslovak Socialist Republic as expressed in the Czechoslovak currency.

8. Germany, the host for the diplomatic conference in 1978, amended the German Commercial Code to apply the Hague-Visby Rules without ratifying or acceding to them.

APPENDIX 3

THE HAGUE RULES

CONTRACTING PARTIES TO THE HAGUE RULES

Algeria (1964)
Angola (1952)
Antigua & Barbuda (1930)
Argentina (1961)
Australia (1955)
Bahamas (1930)
Barbados (1930)
Belgium (1930)
Belize (1930)
Bolivia (1982)
Cape Verde (1952)
Cote d'Ivoire (1961)
Cuba (1930)
Cyprus (1930)
Denmark (1938)
Dominican Republic (1930)
Egypt (1943)
Ecuador (1977)
Fiji (1970)
Finland (1930)
France (1937)
Gambia (1930)
German Democratic Republic (1958)
German Fed. Republic (1953)
Ghana (1930)
Grenada (1930)
Guinea-Bissau (1952)
Guyana (1930)
Hungary (1930)
Ireland (1962)
Islamic Rep. of Iran (1966)
Israel (1959)
Italy (1938)
Jamaica (1930)
Japan (1957)
Kenya (1930)
Kiribati (1930)
Kuwait (1969)
Lebanon (1975)
Madagascar (1965)
Malaysia (1930)
Mauritius (1970)
Monaco (1931)
Mozambique (1952)
Nauru (1955)
Netherlands (1956)
Nigeria (1930)
Norway (1938)
Papua New Guinea (1955)
Paraguay (1967)
Peru (1964)
Poland (1937)
Portugal (1931)
Romania (1937)
Sao Tome and Principe (1952)
Senegal (1978)
Seychelles (1930)
Sierra Leone (1930)
Singapore (1930)
Solomon Islands (1930)
Somalia (1930)
Span (1930)
Sri Lanka (1930)
St Kitts and Nevis (1930)
St Lucia (1930)
St Vincent and the Grenadines (1930)
Sweden (1938)
Switzerland (1954)
Syrian Arab Republic (1974)
Tonga (1930)
Trinidad & Tobago (1930)
Turkey (1955)

Tuvalu (1930)
United Kingdom (1930)
United Republic of Tanzania (1962)
United States of America (1937)
Yugoslavia (1959)
Zaire (1967)

TEXT OF THE HAGUE RULES

Article I. Definitions

In these Rules the following expressions have the meanings hereby assigned to them respectively, that is to say —

(a) "Carrier" includes the owner or the charterer who enters into a contract of carriage with a shipper

(b) "Contract of carriage" applies only to contracts of carriage covered by a bill of lading or any similar document of title, in so far as such document relates to the carriage of goods by sea, including any bill of lading or any similar document as aforesaid issued under or pursuant to a charterparty from the moment at which such bill of lading or similar document of title regulates the relations between a carrier and a holder of the same

(c) "Goods" includes goods, wares, merchandises, and articles of every kind whatsoever, except live animals and cargo which by the contract of carriage is stated as being carried on deck and is so called

(d) "Ship" means any vessel used for the carriage of goods by sea

(e) "Carriage of goods" covers the period from the time when the goods are loaded on to the time when they are discharged from the ship.

Article II. Risks

Subject to the provisions of Article VI, under every contract of carriage of goods by sea the carrier, in relation to the loading, handling, stowage, carriage, custody, care, and discharge of such goods, shall be subject to the responsibilities and liabilities, and entitled to the rights and immunities hereinafter set forth.

Article III. Responsibilities and liabilities

1. The carrier shall be bound, before and at the beginning of the voyage, to exercise due diligence to —

(a) Make the ship seaworthy:

(b) Properly man, equip, and supply the ship:

(c) Make the holds, refrigerating and cool chambers, and all other parts of the ship in which goods are carried, fit and safe for their reception, carriage and preservation.

2. Subject to the provisions of Article IV, the carrier shall properly and carefully load, handle, stow, carry, keep, care for and discharge the goods carried.

3. After receiving the goods into his charge, the carrier, or the master or agent of the carrier, shall, on demand of the shipper, issue to the shipper a bill of lading showing among other things —

(a) The leading marks necessary for identification of the goods as the same are furnished in writing by the shipper before the loading of such goods starts, provided such marks are stamped or otherwise shown clearly upon the goods if uncovered, or on the cases or coverings in which such goods are contained, in such a manner as should ordinarily remain legible until the end of the voyage;

(b) Either the number of packages or pieces, or the quantity, or weight, as the case may be, as furnished in writing by the shipper;

(c) The apparent order and condition of the goods:

Provided that no carrier, master or agent of the carrier, shall be bound to state or show in the bill of lading any marks, number, quantity, or weight which he has reasonable ground for suspecting not accurately to represent the goods actually received, or which he has had no reasonable means of checking.

4. Such a bill of lading shall be *prima facie* evidence of the receipt by the carrier of the goods as therein described in accordance with paragraph 3(a), (b) and (c).

5. The shipper shall be deemed to have guaranteed the carrier the accuracy at the time of shipment of the marks, number, quantity, and weight, as furnished by him, and the shipper shall indemnify the carrier against all loss, damages, and expenses arising or resulting from inaccuracies in such particulars. The right of the carrier to such indemnity shall in no way limit his responsibility and liability under the contract of carriage to any person other than the shipper.

6. Unless notice of loss or damage and the general nature of such loss or damage be given in writing to the carrier or his agent at the port of discharge before or at the time of the removal of the goods into the custody of the person entitled to delivery thereof under the contract of carriage, or, if the loss or damage be not apparent, within three days, such removal shall be *prima facie* evidence of the delivery by the carrier of the goods as described in the bill of lading.

The notice in writing need not be given if the state of the goods has at the time of their receipt been the subject of joint survey or inspection.

In any event the carrier and the ship shall be discharged from all liability in respect of loss or damage unless suit is brought within one year after delivery of the goods or the date when the goods should have been delivered.

In the case of any actual or apprehended loss or damage the carrier and the receiver shall give all reasonable facilities to each other for inspecting and tallying the goods.

7. After the goods are loaded the bill of lading to be issued by the carrier, master or agent of the carrier, to the shipper shall, if the shipper so demands, be a "shipped" bill of lading, provided that if the shipper shall have previously taken up any document of title to such goods, he shall surrender the same as against the issue of the "shipped" bill of lading, but at the option of the carrier such document of title may be noted at the port of shipment by the carrier, master, or agent with the name or names of the ship or ships upon which the goods have been shipped and the date or dates of shipment, and when so noted the same shall for the purpose of this article be deemed to constitute a "shipped" bill of lading.

8. Any clause, covenant or agreement in a contract of carriage relieving the carrier or the ship from liability for loss or damage to or in connection with goods

arising from negligence, fault or failure in the duties and obligations provided in this article or lessening such liability otherwise than as provided in these Rules, shall be null and void and of no effect.

A benefit of insurance or similar clause shall be deemed to be a clause relieving the carrier from liability.

Article IV. Rights and immunities

1. Neither the carrier nor the ship shall be liable for loss or damage arising or resulting from unseaworthiness unless caused by want of due diligence on the part of the carrier to make the ship seaworthy, and to secure that the ship is properly manned, equipped and supplied, and to make the holds, refrigerating and cool chambers and all other parts of the ship in which goods are carried fit and safe for their reception, carriage and preservation in accordance with the provisions of paragraph 1 of Article III. Whenever loss or damage has resulted from unseaworthiness, the burden of proving the exercise of due diligence shall be on the carrier or other person claiming exemption under this section.

2. Neither the carrier nor the ship shall be responsible for loss or damage arising or resulting from —

(a) Act, neglect, or default of the master, mariner, pilot, or the servants of the carrier in the navigation or in the management of the ship:
(b) Fire, unless caused by the actual fault or privity of the carrier:
(c) Perils, dangers and accidents of the sea or other navigable waters:
(d) Act of God:
(e) Act of war:
(f) Act of public enemies:
(g) Arrest or restraint of princes, rulers or people, or seizure under legal process:
(h) Quarantine restrictions:
(i) Act or omission of the shipper or owner of the goods, his agent or representative:
(j) Strikes or lock-outs or stoppage or restraint of labour from whatever cause, whether partial or general:
(k) Riots and civil commotions:
(l) Saving or attempting to save life or property at sea:
(m) Wastage in bulk or weight or any other loss or damage arising from inherent defect, quality, or vice of the goods:
(n) Insufficiency of packing:
(o) Insufficiency or inadequacy of marks:
(p) Latent defects not discoverable by due diligence:
(q) Any other cause arising without the actual fault or privity of the carrier, or without the fault or neglect of the agents or servants of the carrier, but the burden of proof shall be on the person claiming the benefit of this exception to show that neither the actual fault or privity of the carrier nor the

fault or neglect of the agents or servants of the carrier contributed to the loss or damage.

3. The shipper shall not be responsible for loss or damage sustained by the carrier or the ship arising or resulting from any cause without the act, fault or neglect of the shipper, his agents or his servants.

4. Any deviation in saving or attempting to save life or property at sea, or any reasonable deviation shall not be deemed to be an infringement or breach of these Rules or of the contract of carriage, and the carrier shall not be liable for any loss or damage resulting therefrom.

5. Neither the carrier nor the ship shall in any event be or become liable for any loss or damage to or in connection with goods in an amount exceeding 100*l*. per package or unit, or the equivalent of that sum in other currency, unless the nature and value of such goods have been declared by the shipper before shipment and inserted in the bill of lading.

This declaration if embodied in the bill of lading shall be *prima facie* evidence, but shall not be binding or conclusive on the carrier.

By agreement between the carrier, master or agent of the carrier and the shipper another maximum amount than that mentioned in this paragraph may be fixed, provided that such maximum shall not be less than the figure above named.

Neither the carrier nor the ship shall be responsible in any event for loss or damage to or in connection with goods if the nature or value thereof has been knowingly mis-stated by the shipper in the bill of lading.

6. Goods of an inflammable, explosive or dangerous nature to the shipment whereof the carrier, master or agent of the carrier, has not consented, with knowledge of their nature and character, may at any time before discharge be landed at any place or destroyed or rendered innocuous by the carrier without compensation, and the shipper of such goods shall be liable for all damages and expenses directly or indirectly arising out of or resulting from such shipment.

If any such goods shipped with such knowledge and consent shall become a danger to the ship or cargo, they may in like manner be landed at any place or destroyed or rendered innocuous by the carrier without liability on the part of the carrier except to general average, if any.

Article V. Surrender of rights and immunities, and increase of responsibilities and liabilities

A carrier shall be at liberty to surrender in whole or in part all or any of his rights and immunities or to increase any of his responsibilities or liabilities under the Rules contained in any of these articles, provided such surrender or increase shall be embodied in the bill of lading issued to the shipper.

The provisions of these Rules shall not be applicable to charterparties, but if bills of lading are issued in the case of a ship under a charterparty they shall comply with the terms of these Rules. Nothing in these Rules shall be held to prevent the insertion in a bill of lading of any lawful provision regarding general average.

Article VI. Special conditions

Notwithstanding the provisions of the preceding articles, a carrier, master or agent of the carrier, and a shipper shall in regard to any particular goods be at liberty to enter into any agreement in any terms as to the responsibility and liability of the carrier for such goods, and as to the rights and immunities of the carrier in respect of such goods, or his obligation as to seaworthiness, so far as this stipulation is not contrary to public policy, or the care or diligence of his servants or agents in regard to the loading, handling, stowage, carriage, custody, care, and discharge of the goods carried by sea, provided that in this case no bill of lading has been or shall be issued and that the terms agreed shall be embodied in a receipt which shall be a non-negotiable document and shall be marked as such.

Any agreement so entered into shall have full legal effect:

Provided that this article shall not apply to ordinary commercial shipments made in the ordinary course of trade, but only to other shipments where the character or condition of the property to be carried or the circumstances, terms and conditions under which the carriage is to be performed, are such as reasonably to justify a special agreement.

Article VII. Limitations on the application of the Rules

Nothing herein contained shall prevent a carrier or a shipper from entering into any agreement, stipulation, condition, reservation or exemption as to the responsibility and liability of the carrier or the ship for the loss or damage to or in connection with the custody and care and handling of goods prior to the loading on and subsequent to the discharge from the ship on which the goods are carried by sea.

Article VIII. Limitation of liability

The provisions of these Rules shall not affect the rights and obligations of the carrier under any statute for the time being in force relating to the limitation of the liability of owners of sea-going vessels.

Article IX. The gold clause

The monetary units mentioned in these Rules are to be taken to be gold value.

APPENDIX 4

THE HAGUE-VISBY RULES AND UK COGSA 1971

CONTRACTING PARTIES TO THE HAGUE-VISBY PROTOCOL:

Aruba (1986)
Belgium (1987)
Denmark (1975)
Ecuador (1977)
Egypt (1983)
Finland (1984)
France (1977)
German Democratic Republic (1979)
Italy (1985)
Lebanon (1975)
Netherlands (1982)
Norway (1974)
Poland (1980)
Singapore (1972)
Sri Lanka (1981)
Sweden (1974)
Switzerland (1975)
Syrian Arab Republic (1974)
Tonga (1978)
United Kingdom (1976) including Bermuda, Hong Kong and other dependencies

CONTRACTING PARTIES TO THE BRUSSELS PROTOCOL:

Belgium (1983)
Denmark (1983)
Finland (1984)
France (1984)
Italy (1985)
Netherlands (1986)
Norway (1983)
Poland (1984)
Spain (1982)
Sweden (1983)
United Kingdom (1983) including Bermuda, Hong Kong and other dependencies

VISBY AMENDMENT – THE BRUSSELS PROTOCOL 1968

Protocol to amend the International Convention for the Unification of Certain Rules of Law relating to Bills of Lading, signed at Brussels on 25 August 1924

(Brussels, 23 February 1968)

The Contracting Parties,

Considering that it is desirable to amend the International Convention for the unification of certain rules of law relating to bills of lading, signed at Brussels on 25 August 1924,

Have agreed as follows:

Article 1

1. In Article 3, paragraph 4, shall be added:

"However, proof to the contrary shall not be admissible when the bill of lading has been transferred to a third party acting in good faith."

2. In Article 3, paragraph 6, sub-paragraph 4 shall be deleted and replaced by:

"Subject to paragraph 6 *bis* the carrier and the ship shall in any event be discharged from all liability whatsoever in respect of the goods, unless suit is brought within one year of their delivery or of the date when they should have been delivered. This period may, however, be extended if the parties so agree after the cause of action has arisen."

3. In Article 3, after paragraph 6, shall be added the following paragraph 6 *bis*:

"An action for indemnity against a third person may be brought even after the expiration of the year provided for in the preceding paragraph if brought within the time allowed by the law of the court seized of the case. However, the time allowed shall be not less than three months, commencing from the day when the person bringing such action for indemnity has settled the claim or has been served with process in the action against himself."

Article 2

Article 4, paragraph 5, shall be deleted and replaced by the following:

(a) Unless the nature and value of such goods have been declared by the shipper before shipment and inserted in the bill of lading, neither the carrier nor the ship shall in any event be or become liable for any loss or damage to or in connection with the goods in an amount exceeding the equivalent of 10.000 francs per package or unit or 30 francs per kilo of gross weight of the goods lost or damaged, whichever is the higher.

(b) The total amount recoverable shall be calculated by reference to the value of such goods at the place and time at which the goods are discharged from the ship in accordance with the contract or should have been so discharged.

The value of the goods shall be fixed according to the commodity exchange price, or, if there be no such price, according to the current market price, or, if there be no commodity exchange price or current market price, by reference to the normal value of goods of the same kind and quality.

(c) Where a container, pallet or similar article of transport is used to consolidate goods, the number of packages or units enumerated in the bill of lading as packed in such article of transport shall be deemed the number of packages or units for the purpose of this paragraph as far as these packages or units are concerned. Except as aforesaid such article of transport shall be considered the package or unit.

(d) A franc means a unit consisting of 65.6 milligrammes of gold of millesimal fineness 900'. The date of conversion of the sum awarded into national currencies shall be governed by the law of the court seized of the case.

(e) Neither the carrier nor the ship shall be entited to the benefit of the limitation of liability provided for in this paragraph if it is proved that the damage resulted from an act or omission of the carrier done with intent to cause damage, or recklessly and with knowledge that damage would probably result.

(f) The declaration mentioned in sub-paragraph (a) of this paragraph, if embodied in the bill of lading, shall be *prima facie* evidence, but shall not be binding or conclusive on the carrier.

(g) By agreement between the carrier, master or agent of the carrier and the shipper other maximum amounts than those mentioned in sub-paragraph (a) of this paragraph may be fixed, provided that no maximum amount so fixed shall be less than the appropriate maximum mentioned in that sub-paragraph.

(h) Neither the carrier nor the ship shall be responsible in any event for loss or damage to, or in connection with, goods if the nature or value thereof has been knowingly mis-stated by the shipper in the bill of lading."

Article 3

Between Articles 4 and 5 of the Convention shall be inserted the following Article 4 *bis*:

"1. The defences and limits of liability provided for in this Convention shall apply in any action against the carrier in respect of loss or damage to goods covered by a contract of carriage whether the action be founded in contract or in tort.

2. If such an action is brought against a servant or agent of the carrier (such servant or agent not being an independent contractor), such servant or agent shall be entitled to avail himself of the defences and limits of liability which the carrier is entitled to invoke under this Convention.

3. The aggregate of the amounts recoverable from the carrier, and such servants and agents, shall in no case exceed the limit provided for in this Convention.

4. Nevertheless, a servant or agent of the carrier shall not be entitled to avail himself of the provisions of this Article, if it is proved that the damage resulted from an act or omission of the servant or agent done with intent to cause damage or recklessly and with knowledge that damage would probably result."

Article 4

Article 9 of the Convention shall be deleted and replaced by the following:

"This Convention shall not affect the provisions of any international Convention or national law governing liability for nuclear damage."

Article 5

Article 10 of the Convention shall be deleted and replaced by the following:

"The provisions of this Convention shall apply to every bill of lading relating to the carriage of goods between ports in two different States if:

(a) the bill of lading is issued in a Contracting State, or

(b) the carriage is from a port in a Contracting State, or

(c) the Contract contained in or evidenced by the bill of lading provides that the rules of this Convention or legislation of any State giving effect to them are to govern the contract, whatever may be the nationality of the ship, the carrier, the shipper, the consignee, or any other interested person.

Each Contracting State shall apply the provisions of this Convention to the bills of lading mentioned above.

This article shall not prevent a Contracting State from applying the Rules of this Convention to bills of lading not included in the preceding paragraphs."

Article 6

As between the Parties to this Protocol the Convention and the Protocol shall be read and interpreted together as one single instrument.

A Party to this Protocol shall have no duty to apply the provisions of this Protocol to bills of lading issued in a State which is a Party to the Convention but which is not a Party to this Protocol.

Article 7

As between the Parties to this Protocol, denunciation by any of them of the Convention in accordance with Article 15 thereof, shall not be construed in any way as a denunciation of the Convention as amended by this Protocol.

Article 8

Any dispute between two or more Contracting Parties concerning the interpretation or application of the Convention which cannot be settled through negotiation, shall, at the request of one of them, be submitted to arbitration. If within six months from the date of the request for arbitration the Parties are unable to agree on the organisation of the arbitration, any one of those Parties may refer the dispute to the International Court of Justice by request in conformity with the Statute of the Court.

Article 9

1. Each Contracting Party may at the time of signature or ratification of this Protocol or accession thereto, declare that it does not consider itself bound by Article 8 of this Protocol. The other Contracting Parties shall not be bound by this Article with respect to any Contracting Party having made such a reservation.

2. Any Contracting Party having made a reservation in accordance with paragraph 1 may at any time withdraw this reservation by notification to the Belgian Government.

Article 10

This Protocol shall be open for signature by the States which have ratified the Convention or which have adhered thereto before 23 February 1968, and by any State represented at the twelfth session (1967–1968) of the Diplomatic Conference on Maritime Law.

Article 11

1. This Protocol shall be ratified.

2. Ratification of this Protocol by any State which is not a Party to the Convention shall have the effect of accession to the Convention.

3. The instruments of ratification shall be deposited with the Belgian Government.

Article 12

1. States, Members of the United Nations or Members of the specialised agencies of the United Nations, not represented at the twelfth session of the Diplomatic Conference on Maritime Law, may accede to this Protocol.

2. Accession to this Protocol shall have the effect of accession to the Convention.

3. The instruments of accession shall be deposited with the Belgian Government.

Article 13

1. This Protocol shall come into force three months after the date of the deposit of ten instruments of ratification or accession, of which at least five shall have been deposited by States that have each a tonnage equal or superior to one million gross tons of tonnage.

2. For each State which ratifies this Protocol or accedes thereto after the date of deposit of the instrument of ratification or accession determining the coming into force such as is stipulated in §1 of this article, this Protocol shall come into force three months after the deposit of its instrument of ratification or accession.

Article 14

1. Any Contracting State may denounce this Protocol by notification to the Belgian Government.

2. This denunciation shall have the effect of denunciation of the Convention.

3. The denunciation shall take effect one year after the date on which the notification has been received by the Belgian Government.

Article 15

1. Any Contracting State may at the time of signature, ratification or accession or at any time thereafter declare by written notification to the Belgian Government which among the territories under its sovereignty or for whose international relations it is responsible, are those to which the present Protocol applies.

The Protocol shall three months after the date of the receipt of such notification by the Belgian Government extend to the territories named therein, but not before the date of the coming into force of the Protocol in respect of such State.

2. This extension also shall apply to the Convention if the latter is not yet applicable to those territories.

3. Any Contracting State which has made a declaration under §1 of this article may at any time thereafter declare by notification given to the Belgian Government that the Protocol shall cease to extend to such territory. This denunciation shall take effect one year after the date on which notification thereof has been received by the Belgian Government; it also shall apply to the Convention.

Article 16

The Contracting Parties may give effect to this Protocol either by giving it the force of law or by including in their national legislation in a form appropriate to that legislation the rules adopted under this Protocol.

Article 17

The Belgian Government shall notify the States represented at the twelfth session (1967–1968) of the Diplomatic Conference on Maritime Law, the acceding States to this Protocol, and the States Parties to the Convention, of the following:

1. The signatures, ratifications and accessions received in accordance with Articles 10, 11 and 12.

2. The date on which the present Protocol will come into force in accordance with Article 13.

3. The notifications with regard to the territorial application in accordance with Article 15.

4. The denunciations received in accordance with Article 14.

In witness whereof the undersigned Plenipotentiaries, duly authorised, have signed this Protocol.

Done at Brussels, this 23rd day of February 1968, in the French and English languages, both texts being equally authentic, in a single copy, which shall remain deposited in the archives of the Belgian Government, which shall issue certified copies.

(*The signatures*)

HAGUE-VISBY RULES — CARRIAGE OF GOODS BY SEA ACT 1971 AS AMENDED BY THE MERCHANT SHIPPING ACT 1981

An Act to amend the law with respect to the carriage of goods by sea.

[8 April 1971]

Be it enacted by the Queen's most Excellent Majesty, by and with the advice and consent of the Lords Spiritual and Temporal, and Commons, in this present Parliament assembled, and by the authority of the same, as follows:

Application of Hague Rules as amended

1. — (1) In this Act, "the Rules" means the International Convention for the unification of certain rules of law relating to bills of lading signed at Brussels on 25 August 1924, as amended by the Protocol signed at Brussels on 23 February 1968 [and by the Protocol signed at Brussels on 21 December 1979].

(2) The provisions of the Rules, as set out in the Schedule to this Act, shall have the force of law.

(3) Without prejudice to subsection (2) above, the said provisions shall have effect (and have the force of law) in relation to and in connection with the carriage of goods by sea in ships where the port of shipment is a port in the United Kingdom, whether or not the carriage is between ports in two different States within the meaning of Article X of the Rules.

(4) Subject to subsection (6) below, nothing in this section shall be taken as applying anything in the Rules to any contract for the carriage of goods by sea, unless the contract expressly or by implication provides for the issue of a bill of lading or any similar document of title.

(5) The Secretary of State may from time to time by order made by statutory instrument specify the respective amounts which for the purposes of paragraph 5 of Article IV of the Rules and of Article IV *bis* of the Rules are to be taken as equivalent to the sums expressed in francs which are mentioned in sub-paragraph (a) of that paragraph.

(6) Without prejudice to Article X(c) of the rules, the Rules shall have the force of law in relation to —

(a) any bill of lading if the contract contained in or evidenced by it expressly provides that the Rules shall govern the contract, and

(b) any receipt which is a non-negotiable document marked as such if the contract contained in or evidenced by it is a contract for the carriage of goods by sea which expressly provides that the Rules are to govern the contract as if the receipt were a bill of lading, but subject, where paragraph (b) applies, to any necessary modifications and in particular with the omission in Article III of the Rules of the second sentence of paragraph 4 and of paragraph 7.

(7) If and so far as the contract contained in or evidenced by a bill of lading or receipt within paragraph (a) or (b) of subsection (6) above applies to deck cargo or live animals, the Rules as given the force of law by that subsection shall have the effect as if Article 1(c) did not exclude deck cargo and live animals.

In this subsection "deck cargo" means cargo which by the contract of carriage is stated as being carried on deck and is so carried.

Contracting States, etc.

2. — (1) If Her Majesty by Order in Council certifies to the following effect, that is to say, that for the purposes of the Rules —

(a) a State specified in the Order is a contracting State, or is a contracting State in respect of any place or territory so specified; or

(b) any place or territory specified in the Order forms part of a State so specified (whether a contracting State or not), the Order shall, except so far as it has been superseded by a subsequent Order, be conclusive evidence of the matters so certified.

(2) An Order in Council under the section may be varied or revoked by a subsequent Order in Council.

Absolute warranty of seaworthiness not to be implied in contracts to which Rules apply

3. —There shall not be implied in any contract for the carriage of goods by sea to which the Rules apply by virtue of this Act any absolute undertaking by the carrier of the goods to provide a seaworthy ship.

Application of Act to British possessions, etc.

4. — (1) Her Majesty may by Order in Council direct that this Act shall extend, subject to such exceptions, adaptations and modifications as may be specified in the Order, to all or any of the following territories, that is —

(a) any colony (not being a colony for whose external relations a country other than the United Kingdom is responsible),

(b) any country outside Her Majesty's dominions in which Her Majesty has jurisdiction in right of Her Majesty's Government of the United Kingdom.

(2) An Order in Council under this section may contain such transitional and other consequential and incidental provisions as appear to Her Majesty to be expedient, including provisions amending or repealing any legislation about the carriage of goods by sea forming part of the law of any of the territories mentioned in paragraphs (a) and (b) above.

(3) An Order in Council under this section may be varied or revoked by a subsequent Order in Council.

Extension of application of Rules to carriage from ports in British possessions, etc.

5. — (1) Her Majesty may by Order in Council provide that section 1(3) of this Act shall have effect as if the reference therein to the United Kingdom included a reference to all or any of the following territories, that is —

(a) the Isle of Man;

(b) any of the Channel Islands specified in the Order;

(c) any colony specified in the Order (not being a colony for whose external relations a country other than the United Kingdom is responsible);

(d) any associated state (as defined by section 1(3) of the West Indies Act 1967) specified in the Order;

(e) any country specified in the Order, being a country outside Her Majesty's dominions in which Her Majesty has jurisdiction in right of Her Majesty's Government of the United Kingdom.

(2) An Order in Council under this section may be varied or revoked by a subsequent Order in Council.

Supplemental

6. — (1) This Act may be cited as the Carriage of Goods by Sea Act 1971.

(2) It is hereby declared that this Act extends to Northern Ireland.

(3) The following enactments shall be repealed, that is —

(a) the Carriage of Goods by Sea Act 1924,

(b) section 12(4)(a) of the Nuclear Installations Act 1965,

and without prejudice to section 38(1) of the Interpretation Act 1889, the reference to the said Act of 1924 in section 1(*1*)(i)(ii) of the Hovercraft Act 1968 shall include a reference to this Act.

(4) It is hereby declared that for the purposes of Article VIII of the Rules ... [section 18 of the Merchant Shipping Act 1979 (which] entirely exempts shipowners and others in certain circumstances from liability for loss of, or damage to, goods) is a provision relating to limitation of liability.

(5) This Act shall come into force on such day as Her Majesty may by Order in Council appoint, and, for the purposes of the transition from the law in force immediately before the day appointed under this subsection to the provisions of this Act, the Order appointing the day may provide that those provisions shall have effect subject to such transitional provisions as may be contained in the Order.

Schedule. The Hague Rules as Amended by the Brussels Protocol 1968

Article I. Definitions

In these Rules the following words are employed, with the meanings set out below:

(a) "Carrier" includes the owner or the charterer who enters into a contract of carriage with a shipper.

(b) "Contract of carriage" applies only to contracts of carriage covered by a bill of lading or any similar document of title, in so far as such document relates to the carriage of goods by sea, including any bill of lading or any similar document as aforesaid issued under or pursuant to a charterparty from the moment at which such bill of lading or similar document of title regulates the relations between a carrier and a holder of the same.

(c) "Goods" includes goods, wares, merchandise, and articles of every kind whatsoever except live animals and cargo which by the contract of carriage is stated as being carried on deck and is so carried.

(d) "Ship" means any vessel used for the carriage of goods by sea.

(e) "Carriage of goods" covers the period from the time when the goods are loaded on to the time they are discharged from the ship.

Article II. Risks

Subject to the provisions of Article VI, under every contract of carriage of goods by sea the carrier, in relation to the loading, handling, stowage, carriage, custody, care and discharge of such goods, shall be subject to the responsibilities and liabilities, and entitled to the rights and immunities hereinafter set forth.

Article III. Responsibilities and Liabilities

1. The carrier shall be bound before and at the beginning of the voyage to exercise due diligence to —

(a) Make the ship seaworthy.

(b) Properly man, equip and supply the ship.

(c) Make the holds, refrigerating and cool chambers, and all other parts of the ship in which goods are carried, fit and safe for their reception, carriage and preservation.

2. Subject to the provisions of Article IV, the carrier shall properly and carefully load, handle, stow, carry, keep, care for, and discharge the goods carried.

3. After receiving the goods into his charge the carrier or the master or agent of the carrier shall, on demand of the shipper, issue to the shipper a bill of lading showing among other things —

(a) The leading marks necessary for identification of the goods as the same are furnished in writing by the shipper before the loading of such goods starts, provided such marks are stamped or otherwise shown clearly upon the goods if uncovered, or on the cases or coverings in which such goods are contained, in such a manner as should ordinarily remain legible until the end of the voyage.

(b) Either the number of packages or pieces, or the quantity, or weight, as the case may be, as furnished in writing by the shipper.

(c) The apparent order and condition of the goods.

Provided that no carrier, master or agent of the carrier shall be bound to state or show in the bill of lading any marks, number, quantity, or weight which he has reasonable ground for suspecting not accurately to represent the goods actually received, or which he has had no reasonable means of checking.

4. Such a bill of lading shall be *prima facie* evidence of the receipt by the carrier of the goods as therein described in accordance with paragraph 3(a), (b) and (c). However, proof to the contrary shall not be admissible when the bill of lading has been transferred to a third party acting in good faith.

5. The shipper shall be deemed to have guaranteed to the carrier the accuracy at the time of shipment of the marks, number, quantity and weight, as furnished by him, and the shipper shall indemnify the carrier against all loss, damages and expenses arising or resulting from inaccuracies in such particulars. The right of the carrier to such indemnity shall in no way limit his responsibility and liability under the contract of carriage to any person other than the shipper.

6. Unless notice of loss or damage and the general nature of such loss or damage be given in writing to the carrier or his agent at the port of discharge before or at the time of the removal of the goods into the custody of the person entitled to delivery thereof under the contract of carriage, or, if the loss or damage be not apparent, within three days, such removal shall be *prima facie* evidence of the delivery by the carrier of the goods as described in the bill of lading.

The notice in writing need not be given if the state of the goods has, at the time of their receipt, been the subject of joint survey or inspection.

Subject to paragraph 6 *bis* the carrier and the ship shall in any event be discharged from all liability whatsoever in respect of the goods, unless suit is brought within one year of their delivery or of the date when they should have been delivered. This period may, however, be extended if the parties so agree after the cause of action has arisen.

In the case of any actual or apprehended loss or damage the carrier and the receiver shall give all reasonable facilities to each other for inspecting and tallying the goods.

6 *bis*. An action for indemnity against a third person may be brought even after the expiration of the year provided for in the preceding paragraph if brought within the time allowed by the law of the Court seized of the case. However, the time allowed shall be not less than three months, commencing from the day when the person bringing such action for indemnity has settled the claim or has been served with process in the action against himself.

7. After the goods are loaded the bill of lading to be issued by the carrier, master, or agent of the carrier, to the shipper shall, if the shipper so demands, be a "shipped" bill of lading, provided that if the shipper shall have previously taken up any document of title to such goods, he shall surrender the same as against the issue of the "shipped" bill of lading, but at the option of the carrier such document of title may be noted at the port of shipment by the carrier, master, or agent with the name or names of the ship or ships upon which the goods have been shipped and the date or dates of shipment, and when so noted, if it shows the particulars mentioned in paragraph 3 of Article III shall for the purposes of this article be deemed to constitute a "shipped" bill of lading.

8. Any clause, covenant, or agreement in a contract of carriage relieving the carrier or the ship from liability for loss or damage to, or in connection with, goods arising from negligence, fault, or failure in the duties and obligations provided in this article or lessening such liability otherwise than as provided in these Rules, shall be null and void and of no effect. A benefit of insurance in favour of the carrier or similar clause shall be deemed to be a clause relieving the carrier from liability.

Article IV. Right and immunities

1. Neither the carrier nor the ship shall be liable for loss or damage arising or resulting from unseaworthiness unless caused by want of due diligence on the part of the carrier to make the ship seaworthy, and to secure that the ship is properly manned, equipped and supplied, and to make the holds, refrigerating and cool chambers and all other parts of the ship in which goods are carried fit and safe for their reception, carriage and preservation in accordance with the provisions of paragraph 1 of Article III. Whenever loss or damage has resulted from unseaworthiness the burden of proving the exercise of due diligence shall be on the carrier or other person claiming exception under this article.

2. Neither the carrier nor the ship shall be responsible for loss or damage arising or resulting from —

(a) Act, neglect, or default of the master, mariner, pilot, or the servants of the carrier in the navigation or in the management of the ship.
(b) Fire, unless caused by the actual fault or privity of the carrier.
(c) Perils, dangers and accidents of the sea or other navigable waters.
(d) Act of God.
(e) Act of war.
(f) Act of public enemies.
(g) Arrest or restraint of princes, rulers or people, or seizure under legal process.
(h) Quarantine restrictions.
(i) Act or omission of the shipper or owner of the goods, his agent or representative.
(j) Strikes or lockouts or stoppage or restraint of labour from whatever cause, whether partial or general.
(k) Riots and civil commotions.
(l) Saving or attempting to save life or property at sea.
(m) Wastage in bulk or weight or any other loss or damage arising from inherent defect, quality or vice of the goods.
(n) Insufficiency of packing.
(o) Insufficiency or inadequacy of marks.
(p) Latent defects not discoverable by due diligence.
(q) Any other cause arising without the actual fault or privity of the carrier, or without the fault or neglect of the agents or servants of the carrier, but the

burden of proof shall be on the person claiming the benefit of this exception to show that neither the actual fault or privity of the carrier nor the fault or neglect of the agents or servants of the carrier contributed to the loss or damage.

3. The shipper shall not be responsible for loss or damage sustained by the carrier or the ship arising or resulting from any cause without the act, fault or neglect of the shipper, his agents or his servants.

4. Any deviation in saving or attempting to save life or property at sea or any reasonable deviation shall not be deemed to be infringement or breach of these Rules or of the contract of carriage, and the carrier shall not be liable for any loss or damage resulting therefrom.

5. (a) Unless the nature and value of such goods have been declared by the shipper before shipment and inserted in the bill of lading, neither the carrier nor the ship shall in any event be or become liable for any loss or damage to or in connection with the goods in an amount exceeding [666.67 units of account] per package or unit or [2 units of account per kilogramme] of gross weight of the goods lost or damaged, whichever is the higher.

(b) The total amount recoverable shall be calculated by reference to the value of such goods at the place and time at which the goods are discharged from the ship in accordance with the contract or should have been so discharged.

The value of the goods shall be fixed according to the commodity exchange price, or, if there be no such price, according to the current market price, or, if there be no commodity exchange price or current market price, by reference to the normal value of goods of the same kind and quality.

(c) Where a container, pallet or similar article of transport is used to consolidate goods, the number of packages or units enumerated in the bill of lading as packed in such article of transport shall be deemed the number of packages or units for the purpose of this paragraph as far as these packages or units are concerned. Except as aforesaid such article of transport shall be considered the package or unit.

[(d)The unit of account mentioned in this Article is the special drawing right as defined by the International Monetary Fund. The amounts mentioned in sub-paragraph (a) of this paragraph shall be converted into national currency on the basis of the value of that currency on a date to be determined by the law of the Court seized of the case.]

(e) Neither the carrier nor the ship shall be entitled to the benefit of the limitation of liability provided for in this paragraph if it is proved that the damage resulted from an act or omission of the carrier done with intent to cause damage, or recklessly and with knowledge that damage would probably result.

(f) The declaration mentioned in sub-paragraph (a) of this paragraph, if embodied in the bill of lading, shall be *prima facie* evidence, but shall not be binding or conclusive on the carrier.

(g) By agreement between the carrier, master or agent of the carrier and the shipper other maximum amounts than those mentioned in sub-paragraph (a) of this paragraph may be fixed, provided that no maximum amount so fixed shall be less than the appropriate maximum mentioned in that sub-paragraph.

(h) Neither the carrier nor the ship shall be responsible in any event for loss or damage to, or in connection with, goods if the nature or value thereof has been knowingly mis-stated by the shipper in the bill of lading.

6. Goods of an inflammable, explosive, or dangerous nature to the shipment whereof the carrier, master or agent of the carrier has not consented with knowledge of their nature and character, may at any time before discharge be landed at any place, or destroyed or rendered innocuous by the carrier without compensation and the shipper of such goods shall be liable for all damages and expenses directly or indirectly arising out of or resulting from such shipment. If any such goods shipped with such knowledge and consent shall become a danger to the ship or cargo, they may in like manner be landed at any place, or destroyed or rendered innocuous by the carrier without liability on the part of the carrier except to general average, if any.

Article IV *bis*

1. The defences and limits of liability provided for in these Rules shall apply in any action against the carrier in respect of loss or damage to goods covered by a contract of carriage whether the action be founded in contract or in tort.

2. If such an action is brought against a servant or agent of the carrier (such servant or agent not being an independent contractor), such servant or agent shall be entitled to avail himself of the defences and limits of liability which the carrier is entitled to invoke under these Rules.

3. The aggregate of the amounts recoverable from the carrier, and such servants and agents, shall in no case exceed the limit provided for in these Rules.

4. Nevertheless, a servant or agent of the carrier shall not be entitled to avail himself of the provisions of this article, if it is proved that the damage resulted from an act or omission of the servant or agent done with intent to cause damage or recklessly and with knowledge that damage would probably result.

Article V. Surrender of rights and immunities, and increase of responsibilities and liabilities

A carrier shall be at liberty to surrender in whole or in part all or any of his rights and immunities or to increase any of his responsibilities and obligations under these Rules, provided such surrender or increase shall be embodied in the bill of lading issued to the shipper. The provisions of these Rules shall not be applicable to charterparties, but if bills of lading are issued in the case of a ship under a charterparty they shall comply with the terms of these Rules. Nothing in these Rules shall be held to prevent the insertion in a bill of lading of any lawful provisions regarding general average.

Article VI. Special Conditions

Notwithstanding the provisions of the preceding articles, a carrier, master or agent of the carrier and a shipper shall in regard to any particular goods be at liberty to enter into any agreement in any terms as to the responsibility and liability of the carrier for such goods, and as to the rights and immunities of the carrier in respect of such goods, or his obligation as to seaworthiness, so far as this stipulation is not contrary to public policy, or the care or diligence of his servants or agents in regard to the loading, handling, stowage, carriage, custody, care and discharge of the goods carried by sea, provided that in this case no bill of lading has been or shall be issued and that the terms agreed shall be embodied in a receipt which shall be a non-negotiable document and shall be marked as such.

Any agreement so entered into shall have full legal effect.

Provided that this article shall not apply to ordinary commercial shipments made in the ordinary course of trade, but only to other shipments where the character or condition of the property to be carried or the circumstances, terms and conditions under which the carriage is to be performed are such as reasonably to justify a special agreement.

Article VII. Limitations on the application of the Rules

Nothing herein contained shall prevent a carrier or a shipper from entering into any agreement, stipulation, condition, reservation or exemption as to the responsibility and liability of the carrier or the ship for the loss or damage to, or in connection with, the custody and care and handling of goods prior to the loading on, and subsequent to the discharge from, the ship on which the goods are carried by sea.

Article VIII. Limitation of liability

The provisions of these Rules shall not affect the rights and obligations of the carrier under any statute for the time being in force relating to the limitation of the liability of owners of seagoing vessels.

Article IX. Nuclear exclusion

These Rules shall not affect the provisions of any international Convention or national law governing liability for nuclear damage.

Article X. Application

The provisions of these Rules shall apply to every bill of lading relating to the carriage of goods between ports in two different States if:

(a) the bill of lading is issued in a contracting State, or

(b) the carriage is from a port in a contracting State, or

(c) the contract contained in or evidenced by the bill of lading provides that these Rules or legislation of any State giving effect to them are to govern the contract,

whatever may be the nationality of the ship, the carrier, the shipper, the consignee, or any other interested person.

[The last two paragraphs of this article are not reproduced. They require contracting States to apply the Rules to bills of lading mentioned in the article and authorise them to apply the Rules to other bills of lading.]

[Articles 11 to 16 of the International Convention for the unification of certain rules of law relating to bills of lading signed at Brussels on 25 August 1924 are not reproduced. They deal with the coming into force of the Convention, procedure for ratification, accession and denunciation, and the right to call for a fresh conference to consider amendments to the Rules contained in the Convention.]

[*Note*: With effect from 4 February 1984, Special Drawing Rights replaced gold francs as the unit of account for the purpose of Article IV. Under section 3(i) of the Merchant Shipping Act 1981 the value on a particular day of one SDR is to be treated as equal to such sum in Sterling as the International Monetary Fund have fixed as being the equivalent of one SDR for that day or if no sum has been so fixed for that day, for the last day before that day for which a sum has been so fixed. A certificate stating the Sterling equivalent of an SDR on any particular date can be obtained from the UK Treasury on payment of a fee.]

APPENDIX 5

USA COGSA

(49 Stat. 1207–1213 (1936), Title 46 USA paragraphs 1300–1315)

THE CARRIAGE OF GOODS BY SEA ACT

46 USCA § 1300. Bills of lading subject to chapter

Every bill of lading or similar document of title which is evidence of a contract for the carriage of goods by sea to or from ports of the United States, in foreign trade, shall have effect subject to the provisions of this chapter.

§1. (46 USCA § 1301). Definitions

When used in this chapter —

(a) The term "carrier" includes the owner or the charterer who enters into a contract of carriage with a shipper.

(b) The term "contract of carriage" applies only to contracts of carriage covered by a bill of lading or any similar document of title, insofar as such doument relates to the carriage of goods by sea, including any bill of lading or any similar document as aforesaid issued under or pursuant to a charter-party from the moment at which such bill of lading or similar document of title regulates the relations between a carrier and a holder of the same.

(c) The term "goods" includes goods, wares, merchandise, and articles of every kind whatsoever except live animals and cargo which by the contract of carriage is stated as being carried on deck and is so carried.

(d) The term "ship" means any vessel used for the carriage of goods by sea.

(e) The term "carriage of goods" covers the period from the time when the goods are loaded on to the time when they are discharged from the ship.

§2. (46 USCA § 1302). Duties and rights of carrier

Subject to the provisions of section 1306 of this title, under every contract of carriage of goods by sea, the carrier in relation to the loading, handling, stowage, carriage, custody, care, and discharge of such goods, shall be subject to the responsibilities and liabilities and entitled to the rights and immunities set forth in sections 1303 and 1304 of this title.

§3. (46 USCA §1303). Responsibilities and liabilities of carrier and ship

(1) The carrier shall be bound, before and at the beginning of the voyage, to exercise due diligence to —

(a) Make the ship seaworthy;

(b) Properly man, equip, and supply the ship;

(c) Make the holds, refrigerating and cooling chambers, and all other parts of the ship in which goods are carried, fit and safe for their reception, carriage, and preservation.

(2) The carrier shall properly and carefully load, handle, stow, carry, keep, care for, and discharge the goods carried.

(3) After receiving the goods into his charge the carrier, or the master or agent of the carrier, shall, on demand of the shipper, issue to the shipper a bill of lading showing among other things —

(a) The leading marks necessary for identification of the goods as the same are furnished in writing by the shipper before the loading of such goods starts, provided such marks are stamped or otherwise shown clearly upon the goods if uncovered, or on the cases or coverings in which such goods are contained, in such a manner as should ordinarily remain legible until the end of the voyage.

(b) Either the number of packages or pieces, or the quantity or weight, as the case may be, as furnished in writing by the shipper.

(c) The apparent order and condition of the goods: *Provided*, that no carrier, master, or agent of the carrier, shall be bound to state or show in the bill of lading any marks, number, quantity, or weight which he has reasonable ground for suspecting not accurately to represent the goods actually received, or which he has had no reasonable means of checking.

(4) Such a bill of lading shall be *prima facie* evidence of the receipt by the carrier of the goods as therein described in accordance with paragraphs (3)(a), (b), and (c), of this section: *Provided*, that nothing in this chapter shall be construed as repealing or limiting the application any part of sections 81–124 of Title 49.

(5) The shipper shall be deemed to have guaranteed to the carrier the accuracy at the time of shipment of the marks, number, quantity, and weight, as furnished by him; and the shipper shall indemnify the carrier against all loss, damages, and expenses arising or resulting from inaccuracies in such particulars. The right of the carrier to such indemnity shall in no way limit his responsibility and liability under the contract of carriage to any person other than the shipper.

(6) Unless notice of loss or damage and the general nature of such loss or damage be given in writing to the carrier or his agent at the port of discharge before

or at the time of the removal of the goods into the custody of the person entitled to delivery thereof under the contract of carriage, such removal shall be *prima facie* evidence of the delivery by the carrier of the goods as described in the bill of lading. If the loss or damage is not apparent, the notice must be given within three days of the delivery.

Said notice of loss or damage may be endorsed upon the receipt for the goods given by the person taking delivery thereof.

The notice in writing need not be given if the state of the goods has at the time of their receipt been the subject of joint survey or inspection.

In any event the carrier and the ship shall be discharged from all liability in respect of loss or damage unless suit is brought within one year after delivery of the goods or the date when the goods should have been delivered: *Provided*, that if a notice of loss or damage, either apparent or concealed, is not given as provided for in this section, that fact shall not affect or prejudice the right of the shipper to bring suit within one year after the delivery of the goods or the date when the goods should have been delivered.

In the case of any actual or apprehended loss or damage the carrier and receiver shall give all reasonable facilities to each other for inspecting and tallying the goods.

(7) After the goods are loaded the bill of lading to be issued by the carrier, master, or agent of the carrier to the shipper shall, if the shipper so demands, be a "shipped" bill of lading: *Provided*, that if the shipper shall have previously taken up any document of title to such goods, he shall surrender the same as against the issue of the "shipped" bill of lading, but at the option of the carrier such document of title may be noted at the port of shipment by the carrier, master, or agent with the name or names of the ship or ships upon which the goods have been shipped and the date or dates of shipment, and when so noted the same shall for the purpose of this section be deemed to constitute a "shipped" bill of lading.

(8) Any clause, covenant, or agreement in a contract of carriage relieving the carrier or the ship from liability for loss or damage to or in connection with the goods, arising from negligence, fault, or failure in the duties and obligations provided in this section, or lessening such liability otherwise than as provided in this chapter, shall be null and void and of no effect. A benefit of insurance in favour of the carrier, or similar clause, shall be deemed to be a clause relieving the carrier from liability.

§4. (46 USCA §1304). Rights and immunities of carrier and ship

(1) Neither the carrier nor the ship shall be liable for loss or damage arising or resulting from unseaworthiness unless caused by want of due diligence on the part of the carrier to make the ship seaworthy, and to secure that the ship is properly manned, equipped, and supplied, and to make the holds, refrigerating and cool chambers, and all other parts of the ship in which goods are carried fit and safe for their reception, carriage, and preservation in accordance with the provisions of

paragraph (1) of section 1303 of this title. Whenever loss or damage has resulted from unseaworthiness, the burden of proving the exercise of due diligence shall be on the carrier or other persons claiming exemption under this section.

(2) Neither the carrier nor the ship shall be responsible for loss or damage arising or resulting from —

(a) Act, neglect, or default of the master, mariner, pilot, or the servants of the carrier in the navigation or in the management of the ship;
(b) Fire, unless caused by the actual fault or privity of the carrier;
(c) Perils, dangers and accidents of the sea or other navigable waters;
(d) Act of God;
(e) Act of war;
(f) Act of public enemies;
(g) Arrest or restraint of princes, rulers, or people, or seizure under legal process;
(h) Quarantine restrictions;
(i) Act or omission of the shipper or owner of the goods, his agent or representative;
(j) Strikes or lockouts or stoppage or restraint of labour from whatever cause, whether partial or general: *Provided*, that nothing herein contained shall be construed to relieve a carrier from responsibility for the carrier's own acts;
(k) Riots and civil commotions;
(l) Saving or attempting to save life or property at sea;
(m) Wastage in bulk or weight or any other loss or damage arising from inherent defect, quality, or vice of the goods;
(n) Insufficiency of packing;
(o) Insufficiency or inadequacy of marks;
(p) Latent defects not discoverable by due diligence; and
(q) Any other cause arising without the actual fault and privity of the carrier and without the fault or neglect of the agents or servants of the carrier, but the burden of proof shall be on the person claiming the benefit of this exception to show that neither the actual fault or privity of the carrier nor the fault or neglect of the agents or servants of the carrier contributed to the loss or damage.

(3) The shipper shall not be responsible for loss or damage sustained by the carrier or the ship arising or resulting from any cause without the act, fault, or neglect of the shipper, his agents, or his servants.

(4) Any deviation in saving or attempting to save life or property at sea, or any reasonable deviation shall not be deemed to be an infringement or breach of this chapter or of the contract of carriage, and the carrier shall not be liable for any loss or damage resulting therefrom: *Provided, however*, that if the deviation is for the purpose of loading or unloading cargo or passengers it shall, *prima facie*, be regarded as unreasonable.

(5) Neither the carrier nor the ship shall in any event be or become liable for any

loss or damage to or in connection with the transportation of goods in an amount exceeding $500 per package lawful money of the United States, or in case of goods not shipped in packages, per customary freight unit, or the equivalent of that sum in other currency, unless the nature and value of such goods have been declared by the shipper before shipment and inserted in the bill of lading. This declaration, if embodied in the bill of lading, shall be *prima facie* evidence, but shall not be conclusive on the carrier.

By agreement between the carrier, master, or agent of the carrier, and the shipper another maximum amount than that mentioned in this paragraph may be fixed: *Provided*, that such maximum shall not be less than the figure above named. In no event shall the carrier be liable for more than the amount of damage actually sustained.

Neither the carrier nor the ship shall be responsible in any event for loss or damage to or in connection with the transportation of the goods if the nature or value thereof has been knowingly and fraudulently mis-stated by the shipper in the bill of lading.

(6) Goods of an inflammable, explosive, or dangerous nature to the shipment whereof the carrier, master or agent of the carrier, has not consented with knowledge of their nature and character, may at any time before discharge be landed at any place or destroyed or rendered innocuous by the carrier without compensation, and the shipper of such goods shall be liable for all damages and expenses directly or indirectly arising out of or resulting from such shipment. If any such goods shipped with such knowledge and consent shall become a danger to the ship or cargo, they may in like manner be landed at any place, or destroyed or rendered innocuous by the carrier without liability on the part of the carrier except to general average, if any.

§5. (46 USCA § 1305). Surrender of rights; increase of liabilities; charterparties; general average

A carrier shall be at liberty to surrender in whole or in part all or any of his rights and immunities or to increase any of his responsibilities and liabilities under this chapter, provided such surrender or increase shall be embodied in the bill of lading issued to the shipper.

The provisions of this chapter shall not be applicable to charterparties; but if bills of lading are issued in the case of a ship under a charterparty, they shall comply with the terms of this chapter. Nothing in this chapter shall be held to prevent the insertion in a bill of lading of any lawful provision regarding general average.

§6. (46 USCA § 1306). Special agreement as to particular goods

Notwithstanding the provisions of sections 1303–1305 of this title, a carrier, master or agent of the carrier, and a shipper shall, in regard to any particular goods be at liberty to enter into any agreement in any terms as to the responsibility and liability of the carrier for such goods, and as to the rights and immunities of the carrier in respect of such goods, or his obligation as to seaworthiness (so far as the stipulation regarding seaworthiness is not contrary to public policy), or the care or diligence of his servants or agents in regard to the loading, handling, stowage, carriage, custody, care, and discharge of the goods carried by sea: *Provided*, that in this case no bill of lading has been or shall be issued and that the terms agreed shall be embodied in a receipt which shall be a non-negotiable document and shall be marked as such.

Any agreement so entered into shall have full legal effect: *Provided*, that this section shall not apply to ordinary commercial shipments made in the ordinary course of trade but only to other shipments where the character or condition of the property to be carried or the circumstances, terms, and conditions under which the carriage is to be performed are such as reasonably to justify a special agreement.

§7. (46 USCA § 1307). Agreement as to liability prior to loading or after discharge

Nothing contained in this chapter shall prevent a carrier or shipper from entering into any agreement, stipulation, condition, reservation, or exemption as to the responsibility and liability of the carrier or the ship for the loss or damage to or in connection with the custody and care and handling of goods prior to the loading on and subsequent to the discharge from the ship on which the goods are carried by sea.

§8. (46 USCA § 1308). Rights and liabilities under other provisions of Title 46

The provisions of this chapter shall not affect the rights and obligations of the carrier under the provisions of the Shipping Act, 1916, or under the provisions of sections 175, 181–183, and 183b–188 of this title or of any amendments thereto; or under the provisions of any other enactment for the time being in force relating to the limitation of the liability of the owners of seagoing vessels.

§9. (46 USCA § 1309). Discrimination between competing shippers

Nothing contained in this chapter shall be construed as permitting a common carrier by water to discriminate between competing shippers similarly placed in time and circumstances, either (a) with respect to their right to demand and receive bills of lading subject to the provisions of this chapter; or (b) when issuing such bills of lading, either in the surrender of any of the carrier's rights and immunities or in the increase of any of the carrier's responsibilities and liabilities pursuant to section 1305 of this title; or (c) in any other way prohibited by the Shipping Act, 1916, as amended.

§11. (46 USCA § 1310). Weight of bulk cargo

Where under the customs of any trade the weight of any bulk cargo inserted in the bill of lading is a weight ascertained or accepted by a third party other than the carrier or the shipper, and the fact that the weight is so ascertained or accepted is stated in the bill of lading, then, notwithstanding anything in this chapter, the bill of lading shall not be deemed to be *prima facie* evidence against the carrier of the receipt of goods of the weight so inserted in the bill of lading, and the accuracy thereof at the time of shipment shall not be deemed to have been guaranteed by the shipper.

§12. (46 USCA § 1311). Liabilities before loading and after discharge; effect on other laws

Nothing in this chapter shall be construed as superseding any part of sections 190–196 of this title, or of any other law which would be applicable in the absence of this chapter, insofar as they relate to the duties, responsibilities, and liabilities of the ship or carrier prior to the time when the goods are loaded on or after the time they are discharged from the ship.

§13. (46 USCA § 1312). Scope of chapter; "United States"; "foreign trade"

This chapter shall apply to all contracts for carriage of goods by sea to or from ports of the United States in foreign trade. As used in this chapter the term "United States" includes its districts, territories, and possessions. The term "foreign trade" means the transportation of goods between the ports of the United States and ports of foreign countries. Nothing in this chapter shall be held to apply to contracts for carriage of goods by sea between any port of the United States or its possessions, and any other port of the United States or its possessions: *Provided, however*, that any bill of lading or similar document of title which is evidence of a contract for the carriage of goods by sea between such ports, containing an express statement that it shall be subject to the provisions of this chapter, shall be subjected hereto as fully as if subject hereto by the express provisions of this chapter: *Provided further*, that every bill of lading or similar document of title which is evidence of a contract for the carriage of goods by sea from ports of the United States, in foreign trade, shall contain a statement that it shall have effect subject to the provisions of this chapter.

APPENDIX 6

UNCTAD COMMENTS

PART I. GENERAL PROVISIONS

Article 1. Definitions

The definition of "carrier" in Article 1.1 is very general. It stipulates that every person entering into a contract of carriage shall be deemed a carrier, regardless of whether he is an owner or a charterer. The test is merely whether the person contracted with the shipper to transport the goods by sea. Thus, a carrier would include a freight forwarder who contracts with the shipper to transport the goods by sea or a multimodal transport operator subcontracting with an ocean carrier to perform the sea leg of the carriage.

Article 1.2 defines the term "actual carrier". Article 10 makes the "actual carrier" jointly liable with the "contracting carrier" for loss, damage or delay in delivery.

The definition of "shipper" in Article 1.3 is rather broad, covering any person "by whom or in whose name or on whose behalf" a contract of carriage by sea is concluded or whose goods are delivered to a carrier under such a contract.

The definition of "consignee" in Article 1.4 was debated during the preparatory work. It does not add much to the situation under existing law, since the question of what person is entitled to take delivery of the goods will continue to depend on the contract of carriage and the transport document. Furthermore, the definition does not deal with assignees of the cargo, whose rights will have to be resolved under national law. The Hamburg Rules' definition of "goods" is merely illustrative; it does not purport to define all possible types of goods. The definition assumes that the term "goods" is self-explanatory; it specifically incorporates in the definition only certain items which otherwise might be questionable.

The Hamburg Rules define the expression "contract of carriage by sea". Since only a few national legal systems draw a clear distinction between carriage by sea and inland waterway, the term "by sea" and the phrase "from one port to another" in the Rules' definition should not be interpreted too restrictively. The purpose of those words is to support the reference to sea transport. Thus, a "port" may include a port or an inland waterway.

The definition of a "bill of lading" contains only a general description of the document. Articles 14–16 contain additional provisions on bills of lading.

Article 1.8 states that "writing includes, *inter alia*, telegram and telex". By using the word "includes" the drafters intended the reference to telegram and telex to be merely illustrative and not an exclusive listing of all items considered as a "writing". There were some doubts at the Hamburg Conference as to whether telegram and telex should be regarded as writing because they can easily be forged.

However, they were included for practical reasons. For example, Article 19 requires that, to avoid the handing over being considered *prima facie* evidence of delivery in good condition, the consignee must give the carrier written notice of apparent loss or damage not later than the working day after the day the goods were handed over. If a consignee is located a considerable distance from the carrier, he may not be able to rely on a notice sent through the post and may have to give the notice by telegram or telex. It was therefore necessary to ensure that notice by those means is valid.

Article 2. Scope of application

Article 2 covers three aspects relative to the scope of application of the Rules: geographical (Article 2.1) personal (Article 2.2) and substantive (Article 2.3–2.4).

Geographical scope:

The Hamburg Rules are applicable only to the international carriage of goods. This means that carriage between two States is required for the Hamburg Rules to apply. Each contracting State is, of course, free in its national law to extend these Rules to domestic sea carriage as well.

The international carriage of goods need not occur between two Contracting States. It is sufficient that one of the States involved is a Contracting State. The following situations are covered:

1. Either the port of loading or the port of discharge mentioned in the contract is situated in a Contracting State; or,
2. An optional port of discharge mentioned in the contract of carriage which becomes the actual port of discharge is situated in a Contracting State; or,
3. The bill of lading or other document evidencing the contract is issued in a Contracting State; or,
4. The bill of lading or other document evidencing the contract of carriage provides for the application of the Hamburg Rules or any national legislation giving effect to the provisions of the Hamburg Rules.

Personal scope:

Article 2.2 provides that the Hamburg Rules are applicable "without regard to the nationality of the ship, the carrier, the actual carrier, the shipper, the consignee or any other interested person."

Substantive scope:

Article 2.3 excludes charterparties from the scope of the Hamburg Rules. However, the Rules apply to bills of lading issued pursuant to a charterparty when the bill of lading governs the relations between the carrier and a holder of the bill of lading other than the charterer. The third party holder of a bill of lading issued pursuant to a charterparty should have the same protection given to third party holders of other bills of lading, because the person acquiring such a bill of lading is often unable to check the contractual relationship between the carrier and the shipper.

Article 2.4 deals with contracts of carriage in which the carrier undertakes the future carriage of goods in a series of shipments during an agreed period. The paragraph simply states that in such a situation the Hamburg Rules are applicable to each shipment unless the shipment is made under a charterparty, in which case the provisions of Article 2.3 apply.

Article 3. Interpretation of the Convention

Article 3 is an innovation in international transport law. It encourages the Contracting States to promote uniformity of interpretation. The uniform interpretation of internationally agreed uniform rules is, of course, essential if the aim of unification of law is to be reached.

Rules of interpretation of international Conventions differ among various legal systems. Guidance can be found in the Vienna Convention on the Law of Treaties,[1] but it is not very explicit. With respect to the objective of uniformity there is one problem, inherent in many multilateral Conventions, which deserves attention — the fact that the Hamburg Rules have been concluded in six languages, each being equally authentic. Given differences in concepts and terminology in the various legal systems as well as linguistic differences, divergences between the various language versions are practically unavoidable. The question will arise as to how those divergences should be resolved. A possible solution may be found in the Vienna Convention which states that "when a comparison of the authentic text discloses a difference of meaning which the application of Articles 31 and 32 [the general interpretation rules] do not remove, the meaning which best reconciles the texts, having regard to the object and purpose of the treaty, shall be adopted".

In interpreting the Hamburg Rules, it must be borne in mind that they are not a complete code of maritime law. They are meant only to unify the major aspects of the law relating to contracts of carriage by sea. As to other questions not dealt with by the Hamburg Rules, e.g. when damage was caused by the carrier or how the loss should be calculated, it will be necessary to refer to national law.

1. Vienna, 23 May 1969, the Vienna Convention.

PART II. LIABILITY OF THE CARRIER

Article 4. Period of responsibility

Article 4 holds the carrier responsible for the goods during the period in which he is in charge of them. It defines this period as "from the time he (the carrier) has taken over the goods at the port of loading" until the time he has delivered the goods "at the port of discharge". This definition was debated at the Hamburg Conference. It is intended to avoid interference with multimodal transport and to limit the application of the Hamburg Rules to transport by sea. It corresponds to the principle in Article 1.6 that only the ocean part of the carriage is covered by the Hamburg Rules. Thus, if the ocean carrier takes charge of the goods at an inland location, packs them into his container and brings them by rail, road or inland waterway to his vessel at the port, the Hamburg Rules do not apply until arrival of the goods at the port where his ship is loading.

The period of responsibility under the Hamburg Rules is both wider and clearer than that under the Hague Rules. The remaining problems in borderline cases (e.g. those involving carrier and bailee custody in the port) may be solved by courts on the basis of Article 4.2. Pursuant to Article 23 of the Hamburg Rules, the period of responsibility cannot be restricted or reduced.

Article 4.2 is intended for the clarification of the period during which the carrier is in charge of the goods. Mention is made first of the situations where the carrier or his servant or an agent takes over the goods from the shipper or a person acting on his behalf and where he delivers them to the consignee.

With regard to delivery, Article 4.2(b)(ii) expressly mentions the situation where the goods are not received by the consignee but are placed at the disposal of the consignee in accordance with the contract, local law, or usage of the particular trade. The justification for adding this situation is that, if the consignee does not fulfil his obligation to take delivery, the carrier should be relieved of his liability under the Hamburg Rules. This does not mean that he is free of all responsibility for the goods; for example, under national law he may be required to execise reasonable care over them.

Article 4.2(a)(ii) and (b)(iii) deals with an important point concerning the taking over and delivery of the goods. These provisions concern port authorities or other third parties to whom the goods must be handed over before shipment or after discharge in accordance with the laws or regulations of the loading or discharge ports. National laws or regulations frequently grant monopolies to State owned or private warehouses or docks for handling and storage of goods, particularly in connection with customs procedures.

The policy of these provisions is that, if the carrier is not free to choose such a facility, he should not be liable for damage to the goods caused by the facility. Article 4.2(b)(iii) states that he is not in charge of the goods in those circumstances.

While the provisions of Article 4.2(a)(ii) and (b)(iii) seem sound, they may result in difficulties where local law allows a shipper or carrier to choose between two or more authorised facilities to handle the goods.

Article 4.3 makes clear that reference in the article to the carrier or consignee includes servants or agents acting on their behalf. Article 4.2(a)(i) applies the same principle in respect of the shipper.

Article 5. Basis of liability

Preliminary comments on articles 5–8

Articles 5–8 constitute a compromise reconciling divergent views expressed during the preparation of the Hamburg Rules as to the carrier's liability. A minority favoured retaining the exception in for the "act, neglect or default of the master, mariner, pilot or servants of the carrier in the navigation or in the management of the ship".

The vast majority, however, felt that the exception for this so-called "nautical default" was no longer justified, particularly since it had no parallel in other fields of law relating to transport. The compromise between these points of view was to delete the nautical fault exception but to set the limits of liability of the carrier at relatively low amounts (only slightly above those of the Visby Protocol) and to allow the limits of liability to be broken only in case of the carrier's serious misconduct. Another element of the compromise was to create an exception to the "presumed fault" basis on the carrier's liability by requiring the claimant to prove the carrier's fault or neglect in the case of loss, damage or delay in delivery caused by fire.

Article 5 adopts the principle of presumed fault or neglect. The carrier is liable for loss resulting from loss or damage to the goods or delay in delivery in respect of the goods if the occurrence causing the loss, damage or delay in delivery took place while the goods were in the care of the carrier, unless the carrier proves that he and his servants or agents took all measures which he could reasonably be required to take to avoid the occurrence which caused the loss, damage or delay in delivery and its consequences.

Since Article 5.1 makes the carrier liable not only for loss of or damage to the goods but also for "delay in delivery" it was necessary to establish what constituted delay. Article 5.2 provides that delay in delivery occurs, first "when the goods have not been delivered … within the time expressly agreed upon". Non-compliance with an agreed delivery date term is thus obviously non-fulfilment of the contract by the carrier. Secondly, Article 5.2 also provides that if the contract does not mention an exact delivery time or period, the goods must be delivered within "the time which it would be reasonable to require of a diligent carrier, having regard to the circumstances of the case".

Article 5.3 deals with a situation that is also dealt with in most other transport Conventions. A cargo owner claiming against a carrier for the loss of the goods may encounter a problem in proving that the goods were lost, rather than merely delayed. For such situations, Article 5.3 provides that if the goods have not been delivered within 60 days from the time when they should have been delivered, they may be treated as lost.

The problem dealt with in Article 5.3 is not of the greatest practical importance, since it is possible for the carrier to provide for very generous delivery dates in his bill of lading. Nevertheless, the rule facilitates formal claims. However, it does not provide a solution to the problems occurring when the goods are found later on. Other Conventions have dealt with this problem, For example, Article 30 of the CIM[2] provides that in such a case the consignee may insist upon delivery after repayment of the compensation already made by the carrier.

Paragraph 4: Fire

Pursuant to Article 5.4, when loss, damage or delay in delivery results from fire, the presumption of fault on the part of the carrier or his servants or agents provided for in Article 5.1 does not apply.

The majority of the participants of the Hamburg Conference thought it reasonable to place the burden of proof of fault on the claimant, especially as fires aboard ship frequently originate from the cargo.

This view was adopted in the context of the overall compromise, referred to above, with respect to the system of liability under the Hamburg Rules.

Paragraph 5: Live animals

Article 5.5 deals with the carriage of live animals. It exempts the carrier from liability for any loss, damage or delay in delivery resulting from any special risk inherent in the carriage of live animals. If the carrier establishes that he complied with the shipper's special instructions and there is no proof that the loss or damage resulted from the carrier's fault or neglect, it will be presumed that any loss, damage or delay in delivery resulted from those special risks. If the presumption is not rebutted by contrary proof, the carrier will be exempt from liability for the loss, damage or delay in delivery. In other cases, the ordinary rules on liability set forth in Article 5.1 apply.

Paragraph 6: Salvage measures

Article 5.6 provides that the carrier will not be liable, except in general average, for loss, damage or delay in delivery resulting from measures to save life. However, in the case of measures to save property, the measures taken must be reasonable if the carrier is to be exonerated from liability.

Paragraph 7: Causation of damage

Pursuant to Article 5.7 the carrier is not liable under the Hamburg Rules to the extent he proves that the damage or part thereof is not attributable to his (or his servants' or agents') fault or neglect.

2. International Convention Concerning the Carriage of Goods by Rail (CIM) (Bern, 7 February 1970).

In practice, however, this may cause difficulties in interpretation because different legal regimes adopt different theories on joint causation.

The Hamburg Rules provision may not give clear guidelines when the proportion of damages attributable to one or another cause cannot be definitely identified. However, the provision gives general guidance to courts and arbitral tribunals as to how to deal with the problem.

Article 6. Limits of liability

Paragraph 1: Principle

Article 6.1 establishes limits of liability of the carrier for loss of or damage to the goods. The claimant is limited to the higher of two alternatives under the Hamburg Rules. The first alternative is based on the package or other shipping unit; here the maximum liability is an amount equal to 835 "units of account" per package or other shipping unit. The second alternative is based on the gross weight of the goods lost or damaged; here the maximum liability is an amount equal to 2.5 "units of account" per kilogramme of gross weight of the goods. Article 26 provides that the "unit of account" mentioned in Article 6 is, for most States, the Special Drawing Right (SDR)[3] as defined by the International Monetary Fund.

Article 6.1(b) establishes the limits of liability of the carrier for delay in delivery equal to two and a half times the freight payable for the goods delayed, but not exceeding the total freight payable under the contract of carriage of goods by sea. Pursuant to Article 6.1(c), the total liability of the carrier for loss, damage and delay in delivery may in no case exceed the maximum limit for the total loss of goods under Article 6.1(a).

Paragraph 2: Application of the per package rule

Article 6.2(a) sets forth a rule for determining the number of packages or shipping units for the purpose of applying the per package limitation in Article 6.1(a). If a container, pallet or similar article of transport is used to consolidate goods, the packages or shipping units are those enumerated in the document evidencing the contract of carriage by sea. Under Article 6.2(b) the container itself is considered an additional separate shipping unit if it is not owned or otherwise supplied by the carrier. Thus, if a bill of lading enumerates 10 packages in a shipper-supplied container, and all 10 packages as well as the container are damaged, 11 units are considered to have been damaged.

The carrier may insert a reservation in the bill of lading by a clause stating, for example, "shipper's load, count and seal. Carrier has had no means of checking number of packages."

3. Authors' footnote: the composition of the SDR is a trade weighted basket of currencies composed in March 1995 of: United States: 36.65%; Germany: 21.0%; Japan: 23.38%; United Kingdom: 8.4%; France: 10.57%.

Paragraph 4: Agreements

The Hamburg Rules allow the carrier and shipper to agree to limits of liability which are higher than those provided for in the Rules. Article 6.4 reflects the general principle set out in Article 23.2 that the carrier may increase his responsibilities and obligations under the Hamburg Rules. This provision was inserted because agreements to increase the limit of liability are found in practice, although they are rather unusual because of the existence of cargo insurance.

Article 7. Application to non-contractual claims

Paragraph 1: Actions against the carrier

Contractual clauses providing for specific liabilities, limits and defences fulfil their purpose only if a claiming party is unable to make additional claims based on national tort law or other national laws. Under Article 7.1 the defences and limits of liability specified in the Rules apply to any claim for loss, damage or delay in delivery in respect of goods covered by the contract of carriage, whatever its nature.

Paragraph 2: Himalaya clause

Article 7.2 extends to agents and servants of the carrier the benefits of the defences and limits of liability which are available to the carrier under the Hamburg Rules when they act within the scope of their employment by the carrier.

Claims against servants and agents of the carrier are normally actions in tort, because the servants and agents are not parties to the contract. This rule is intended to protect the carrier. Without such a provision, cargo interests could be entitled to claim compensation under national law from agents and servants of the carrier in cases where the carrier would be able to disclaim liability owing to his ability to invoke defences under the Hamburg Rules, or the cargo interests might be able to claim higher amounts of compensation than could be recovered from the carrier under the Hamburg Rules. The carrier might be bound under his contract with the agents or servants to hold them harmless from claims by cargo interests. Thus, without a provision such as that in Article 7.2, the carrier could be indirectly subject to liabilities beyond those contained in the Hamburg Rules.

The Rules do not include the exclusion of independent contractors because to do so was regarded as superfluous and even ambiguous. "Independent contractor" is primarily a common law term; however, in the common law systems servants and agents are never independent contractors.

Paragraph 3: Aggregate of amounts recoverable

If the carrier and his servants or agents are jointly liable for loss, damage or delay in delivery, the total amount recoverable by a claimant cannot exceed the limits of liability provided for in the Hamburg Rules.

Without such a provision, a claimant might be able to obtain multiple recoveries from the carrier and from his servants and agents. A carrier who agrees to hold his servants and agents harmless against claims by cargo interests would thus be exposed to liability for loss, damage or delay in delivery in excess of the amounts stipulated in the Hamburg Rules.

Article 8. Loss of right to limit responsibility

Paragraph 1: Right of the carrier

According to Article 8.1 the carrier may not limit his liability if the loss, damage or delay in delivery resulted from the carrier's act or omission done with intent to cause such loss, damage or delay or done recklessly and with knowledge that such loss, damage or delay in delivery would probably result (hereinafter referred to as "serious misconduct").

Paragraph 2: Right of servants or agents

Since Article 7.2 gives servants and agents an independent right to invoke limitation of liability under the Rules, Article 8.2 provides that they lose the right to invoke the limits in the event of their own serious misconduct.

Article 9. Deck cargo

Paragraph 1: Principle

Carriage of cargo on deck exposes the cargo to higher risks of damage than carriage under deck. Therefore, Article 9.1 provides that the carrier is entitled to carry goods on deck only in accordance with an agreement with the shipper or the usage of the particular trade or if required by statutory rules or regulations (e.g., regulations requiring the carriage of dangerous goods on deck). In such cases, the carrier is liable for damage in accordance with Article 5.1 and is entitled to raise the defence that he, his servants and agents took all measures that could reasonably be required to avoid the occurrence causing the loss, damage or delay in delivery and its consequences. If, however, the carrier is not allowed to carry the goods on deck, he will be liable for loss, damage or delay in delivery resulting solely from the carriage on deck; he will not be entitled to raise the defence just mentioned, but his liability will be limited in accordance with Articles 6 and 8.

Deck cargo under the Hamburg Rules is subject to the same liability regime as all other kinds of cargo. The Hamburg Rules greatly contribute to clarifying when the carrier will be entitled to carry goods — in particular containers — on deck. Clauses in the contract of carriage by sea permitting him so to do will be sufficient.

With respect to deck cargo, the Hamburg Conference decided not to impose on the cargo interests the burden of proving the fault or neglect of the carrier, his servants or agents, as it had done in Article 5.5 for carriage of live animals.

Paragraph 2: Proof of agreement

Article 9.2 adds certain rules relative to an agreement between the parties that goods shall or may be carried on deck. The carrier must insert a statement of the agreement in the bill of lading or other document evidencing the contract of carriage by sea. In the absence of such a statement, the carrier has the burden of proving the existence of such an agreement. Such an agreement cannot be invoked against a third party. However, under Article 9.1, even if a statement of the agreement has not been inserted, the carrier may carry cargo on deck if such carriage is in accordance with the usage of the particular trade or is required by statutory rules or regulations.

Paragraphs 3 and 4: Liability

As discussed above, liability for loss, damage or delay in delivery in respect of deck cargo is the same as liability for all other kinds of cargo (i.e. in accordance with Articles 5, 6 and 8). However, Article 9.3 and 9.4 provide exceptions where carriage on deck has not been justified.

Article 10. Liability of the carrier and actual carrier

Paragraph 1: Contracting carrier

According to Article 10.1, if the carrier who contracts with the shipper (the contracting carrier) entrusts the carriage, or part of it, to another carrier (the actual carrier), the contracting carrier remains liable for loss, damage or delay in delivery in respect of the goods during the entire carriage regardless of his agreement with the actual carrier. Moreover, the contracting carrier is responsible for the acts or omissions of the actual carrier, his servants and agents acting within the scope of their employment.

Paragraph 2: Actual carrier

Article 10.2 makes the actual carrier liable in respect of the carriage performed by him to the cargo interests to the same extent as the contractual carrier. This principle is of great practical importance. Pursuant to Article 10.4, the liability of the contracting carrier and the actual carrier is joint and several. This follows the pattern of air law set out in the Guadalajara Convention.[4]

The liability of the actual carrier does not depend on specific stipulations to that effect in the contract of carriage or transport document; it is derived from the Hamburg Rules themselves.

The actual carrier is responsible only for the part of the carriage entrusted to him. The Hamburg Conference decided against making the actual carrier jointly

4. Guadalajara Convention: Convention supplementary to the Warsaw Convention for the Unification of Certain Rules relating to International Carriage by Air performed by a Person other than the Contracting Carrier (Guadalajara, 18 September 1961).

responsible with the contracting carrier for the entire carriage, since this would have gone too far. To hold the actual carrier liable under the Hamburg Rules, the cargo interest must prove that the damage occurred during the portion of the carriage performed by the actual carrier.

Article 10.3 to 10.6 contains certain additional rules of a more technical nature. Article 10.3 indicates that any special agreement under which the carrier assumes obligations not imposed by the Hamburg Rules, or waives rights conferred on him by the Rules, will not affect the actual carrier unless he agrees expressly and in writing. Article 10.4 states that where and to the extent that both the contracting and actual carrier are liable their liability is joint and several. Article 10.5 provides the maximum amount recoverable from both the contracting and actual carrier shall not exceed the limits of liability under the Hamburg Rules. Article 10.6 provides that nothing in Article 10 shall prejudice a right of recourse between the contracting and actual carriers. Thus, under the Hamburg Rules, the contracting and actual carriers are free to agree as to how to allocate between themselves their joint responsibility to the cargo interest.

Article 11. Through carriage

Paragraph 1: Principle

Article 11.1 enables the contracting carrier, in the contract of carriage, to exclude his liability for loss, damage and delay in delivery attributable to the actual carrier in certain cases of transport, i.e. performance of the carriage by two or more successive sea carriers. The contract of carriage by sea must explicitly provide that a specified part of the carriage is to be performed by someone other than the carrier. Moreover, the actual carrier must be expressly named in the contract, and it must be possible to institute judicial proceedings under the Hamburg Rules against the actual carrier in a court competent under Article 21.1 and 21.2. The burden of proving that the loss, damage or delay in delivery was caused by an occurrence during the actual carriage rests with the carrier.

Article 11 is an exception to Article 10. It does not deal with multimodal transport. Article 11 will help safeguard cargo interests for several reasons. First, it maintains the liability of the contractual carrier in respect of periods of transport when the actual carrier is not in charge of the goods, e.g. during transhipment or temporary storage within a port. Secondly, it requires the actual carrier to be expressly named in the contract, thus enabling the cargo interests to identify him.

Thirdly, and most importantly, it ensures that the contracting carrier will be able to exclude his liability only if the claimant can institute proceedings against the actual carrier.

Paragraph 2: Liability of actual carrier

Article 11.2 makes the actual carrier responsible in accordance with the provisions of Article 10.2 for loss, damage or delay in delivery caused by an occurrence taking place while the goods are in his charge. This completes the scheme of joint and several liability of the contractual and actual carriers and is a useful clarification.

PART III. LIABILITY OF THE SHIPPER

Article 12. General rule

Article 12 regulates the liability of the shipper for loss sustained by the contracting or actual carrier for damage to the ship. Like the carrier's liability, the shipper's liability is based on the fault or neglect committed by himself, his servants or agents.

Article 13. Special rules on dangerous goods

Paragraph 1: Labelling of dangerous goods

Article 13.1 states that the shipper must mark or label dangerous goods as dangerous. This must be done in a suitable manner. Rules concerning the marking and labelling of dangerous goods are imposed in international Conventions on the subject and in national law.

Paragraph 2: Shipper's duty to inform the carrier of the dangerous cargo

Article 13.2 requires the shipper to inform the carrier of the dangerous character of the goods and, if necessary, of the precautions to be taken. In case of non-compliance with this requirement the carrier is entitled to recover compensation from the shipper for any loss sustained as a result of carrying the dangerous cargo, as well as to unload, destroy or render innocuous the cargo without payment of compensation.

Paragraph 3: Carrier's knowledge of the dangerous nature of the cargo

Article 13.3 states that the carrier may not invoke the rights under Article 13.2 if he took over the goods with knowledge of the dangerous character of the goods. This provision is useful because it clarifies that the carrier may not benefit from those provisions if, at the time he takes over the goods, he has knowledge from any source of their dangerous character, even if the shipper failed to give him complete particulars pursuant to Article 13.1.

Paragraph 4: The carrier's right to take action

The carrier may unload, destroy or render innocuous dangerous goods if they become an actual danger to life or property. In such situations the carrier need not pay compensation unless he is liable under Article 5 for fault or has an obligation to contribute in general average.

Nothing is said in the Hamburg Rules about the carrier's right to ask for payment of freight in these cases. The Hamburg Conference was of the opinion that a provision to that effect was unnecessary as most legal systems hold the shipper liable for freight and expenses where the non-performance of the contract is caused by a failure of the shipper to provide relevant information to the carrier or by specific characteristics of the cargo. Moreover, provisions in the contract relating to freight will govern the situation; such clauses are not affected by the Hamburg Rules which do not interfere with contractual provisions which are not in conflict with the Rules.

PART IV. TRANSPORT DOCUMENTS

Article 14. Issue of bill of lading

Paragraph 1: Right to demand a bill of lading

Article 14.1 requires the carrier to issue to the shipper a bill of lading when so demanded by the shipper. If the shipper does not demand a bill of lading, the carrier may issue another document (e.g., a sea waybill).

Paragraph 2: Signing of the bill of lading

While the first sentence of this paragraph is self-evident, the second sentence adds a useful rule of interpretation: a bill of lading signed by the master of the ship carrying the goods is deemed to have been signed on behalf of the carrier. This may help to clarify situations which under present practices are uncertain. This clarification will be especially useful in cases where the contracting carrier entrusts part or all of the carriage to an actual carrier.

Paragraph 3: Signature

Article 14.3 attempts to clarify the term "signature" by giving a list of examples. These extend the meaning of "signature" to cover, in addition to handwritten signatures, signatures by any other means, mechanical, electronic or otherwise, so long as they are not inconsistent with the law of the country where the bill of lading is issued.

This was made to facilitate the transfer of documents, including their signature, by electronic means, a fact which is becoming increasingly important given the greater use of electronic data interchange.

Article 15. Contents of bill of lading

Paragraph 1: List of contents

Article 15.1 provides a list of items which "must" be included in the bill of lading.

Article 15.3 then modifies somewhat this obligation since failure to include one or more of the particulars mentioned in Article 15.1 will not affect the legal character of the bill of lading. To do so would put too great a burden on commercial transactions. The term "must" in Article 15.1 means only that if a bill of lading does not contain the required particulars, the carrier is in violation of the contract of carriage. As will be discussed in connection with Article 16, the omission of certain particulars may also have certain evidentiary effects.

Article 15.1(a) requires that the number of packages or pieces as well as the weight of the goods be shown in the bill of lading. In practice there may be no means available of checking the weight of the goods; in such cases the carrier must make a reservation under Article 16.1 specifying the absence of reasonable means of checking. Such a reservation will not affect the commercial value of the bill of lading or render the bill of lading "unclean" in the sense of the rules on documentary credits.

Article 15.1(f) requires the inclusion in the bill of lading of the name and principal place of business of the carrier. This is to identify the issuer of the bill of lading, since it is important that the bill of lading identifies as clearly as possible the contracting party and where he can be found. Indicating the principal place of business of the carrier will also establish one of the places in which a claim can be brought against the carrier in accordance with Article 21.1(a) and 21.3. Of course, a "shipped" bill of lading will identify the ship, which may provide sufficient information to the shipper, at least for the purposes of an action *in rem*. However, a carrier may issue a "received for shipment" bill of lading which, under the Hamburg Rules, has the same economic value as a "shipped on board" bill of lading.

Article 15.1(f) requires the inclusion in the bill of lading of the port of loading and the date of the carrier's taking charge. Such particulars are normally shown in a bill of lading for commercial purposes: a person who acquires a bill of lading needs to know where and when the carrier took charge of the goods.

Article 15.1(k) requires the inclusion in the bill of lading of a statement as to the freight paid to the extent this is payable by the consignee. There was some discussion during the preparation of the Hamburg Rules of requiring the bill of lading to state the amount of freight payable by the consignee. However, since it is not always possible to show the exact amount of freight that was not prepaid, it is sufficient under the Hamburg Rules, to indicate in the bill of lading that freight is payable by the consignee. This should give sufficient protection to a transferee of the bill of lading. Under Article 16.4, if the bill of lading does not indicate that freight is payable by the consignee, this is *prima facie* evidence that no such freight is payable by him. Moreover, proof that freight is payable is not admissible against a good faith transferee of the bill of lading who relied on the absence of an indication in the bill of lading that the freight was payable.

Article 15.1(l) requires inclusion in the bill of lading of a statement that the contract is subject to the Hamburg Rules which nullify any stipulation detracting therefrom to the detriment of the shipper or the consignee. The requirement that the bill of lading indicates that the carriage is subject to the Hamburg Rules will help to ensure that the provisions referred to in that statement will govern the carriage even in States that are not parties to the Rules. The requirement in Article 15.1(l) is somewhat similar to provisions in other international Conventions. For example, Article 8(c) of the Protocol to amend the Warsaw Convention of 12 October 1919 for the Unification of Certain Rules relating to International Carriage by Air,[5] requires a statement to the effect that the Warsaw Convention may be applicable to the air carriage and imposes, in Article 9 (which has not been adopted in the Hamburg Rules), that, in the absence of that statement, the carrier may not invoke the limits of liability under the Convention. The CMR[6] also requires a statement that the carriage is subject to that Convention. Under Article 7.3 of the CMR, the carrier is liable for all expenses, loss and damage sustained by the person entitled to dispose of the goods as a result of the omission of the statement. The sanction under the Hamburg Rules (Article 23.4) for a failure to include the statement is that the carrier must compensate the claimant to the extent provided for under the Hamburg Rules if the claimant incurs a loss as a result of the omission of the statement. In addition, the carrier must compensate the claimant for the cost incurred by him in exerising his right to compensation under the Hamburg Rules where, for example, the Rules have not been applied owing to the omission of the statement.

Paragraph 2: Shipped bill of lading

If the shipper demands a "shipped" bill of lading after the goods have been loaded, the carrier must issue one. If the carrier has already issued a "received for shipment" bill of lading or other document of title with respect to the goods, the shipper must surrender that document in exchange for a shipped bill of lading if the carrier so requests. Instead of issuing a separate, new document, the carrier may amend the previously issued bill of lading (e.g., by stamping "shipped on board the vessel"), provided that such a bill of lading includes all the information required for a "shipped" bill of lading.

The importance of a "shipped" bill of lading will probably decrease under the Hamburg Rules because, in contrast to the Hague Rules, the carrier will be liable from the moment he has taken the goods in charge in the port of loading.

Although, traditionally, a "shipped bill of lading" added the important commercial fact that the goods had been taken on board a specified ship, this need will diminish with the greater use of the new ICCUDP[7] which no longer require a "shipped" bill of lading.

5. The Hague, 28 September 1955, the Hague Protocal.

6. International Carriage of Goods by Road, CMR (Geneva, 19 May 1956).

7. International Chamber of Commerce Uniform Documentary Practices, ICC Brochure 400 in operation as of 1.10.1984 which provides: "The description of the goods in the commercial invoice must correspond with the description in the credit. In all other documents, the goods may be described in general terms not inconsistent with the description of the goods in the credit." It is clear from the wording that the bills of lading as "other documents" need only to state "general terms".

Paragraph 3: Validity

Article 15.3 provides that the absence of one or more of the particulars listed in Article 15.1 does not affect the legal character of a bill of lading provided that it meets the requirements referred to in Article 1.7.

Article 16. Bills of lading: reservations and evidentiary effect

Paragraph 1: Reservations

Article 16.1 requires the carrier to insert a reservation if:

(a) he knows or has reasonable grounds to suspect certain inaccuracies in the bill of lading description of the goods taken over or loaded, or

(b) he had no reasonable means of checking such particulars.

The reservation must specify the inaccuracies, grounds of suspicion or absence of reasonable means of checking.

The Hamburg Rules, unlike the Hague Rules, require the carrier, master or carrier's agent to specify the grounds for suspicion as to the inaccuracy of the particulars and the absence of reasonable means of checking. For example, if there are no facilities for weighing the cargo, this must be stated.

The wording of the Hamburg Rules provision — i.e. that the carrier "must" insert the reservation — may be somewhat misleading, as there is no direct sanction if he does not conform with this requirement. However, if he does not insert a reservation, the bill of lading is *prima facie* evidence of taking over or loading of the goods as described therein. Proof that the goods were not in fact as stated in the bill of lading will not be admissible if the bill of lading has been transferred to a third party, including a consignee, who in good faith has acted in reliance on the description of the goods in the bill of lading.

Paragraph 2: Presumption of apparent good condition

Article 16.2 provides that if the bill of lading does not note the apparent condition of the goods, it is deemed to note that they were in apparent good condition.

Paragraph 3: Evidence

Except in respect of reservations permitted under Article 16.1, a bill of lading is *prima facie* evidence of taking over or, as the case may be, loading of the goods described in the bill of lading. Article 16.3(b) provides that proof to the contrary by the carrier is not admissible if a bill of lading has been acquired by a third party who has in good faith acted in reliance on the description therein.

Paragraph 4: Evidence of payment of freight

Article 16.4 provides that, if the bill of lading does not indicate that freight is payable by the consignee, as required in Article 15.1(k), or set forth demurrage incurred at the port of loading payable by the consignee, the bill of lading is *prima facie* evidence that no such freight or demurrage is payable by the consignee. Proof to the contrary is not admissible against a third party transferee who in good faith has acted in reliance on the absence in the bill of lading of any indication as to the freight payable.

Article 17. Guarantees by the shipper

Paragraph 1: Guarantee of accuracy of indications

Under Article 17.1 the shipper is deemed to have guaranteed to the carrier the accuracy of certain particulars furnished by him for insertion in the bill of lading. The shipper must indemnify the carrier against losses resulting from inaccuracies in such particulars. This includes, for example, extra costs incurred by the carrier as a result of the improper stowage or delivery of the goods owing to wrong information in the bill of lading. Losses by the carrier arising from wrong information concerning dangerous goods are dealt with in Article 13.

Paragraphs 2–4: Letters of guarantee

In practice, shippers sometimes demand a "clean" bill of lading (i.e. without reservations) even though the carrier may have grounds to question the accuracy of the information supplied by the shipper for insertion in the bill of lading or may have no reasonable means of checking that information, or may have discovered defects in the condition of the goods. If this is the case, the shipper may, in return, offer to provide the carrier with a letter of guarantee indemnifying the carrier against loss suffered by him as a result of issuing the "clean" bill of lading. Such guarantees serve a commercial purpose by enabling sales transactions requiring a "clean" bill of lading to take place and by promoting the movements of goods. The prevailing view at the Hamburg Conference was that such guarantees ought to be given legitimacy. However, provisions were included to protect against the use of such letters of guarantee to defraud the consignee. Article 17 sets forth the following principles:

(a) Article 17.2 makes a letter of guarantee by the shipper to the carrier without effect as against a third party. This principle probably did not need to be expressed because the third party obviously is not a party to the contract of guarantee. Nevertheless, it was set forth for the sake of clarity.

(b) Article 17.3 contains perhaps the rule of main importance: a letter of guarantee is valid against a shipper unless the carrier, by omitting a reservation, intends to defraud a third party who acts in reliance on the description of the goods in the bill of lading. Furthermore, if the omitted reservation relates to particulars furnished by the shipper for insertion in the bill of lading, the carrier loses his right of indemnity against the shipper for loss resulting from inaccuracies in those particulars.

(c) Article 17.4 adds another sanction against the carrier acting with intent to defraud: the carrier is liable for loss incurred by a third party acting in reliance on the description of the goods in the bill of lading, and the carrier is not entitled to invoke the limits of liability under the Hamburg Rules.

Questions arise where the carrier may not have had actual knowledge of a fraud committed by the shipper, but should have known of the fraud. The Hamburg Rules do not expressly deal with this situation because many delegations feared that to subject the carrier to sanctions in such cases could interfere with normal trade practices and usages.

In those national jurisdictions that treat letters of guarantee even more strictly than do the Hamburg Rules, present national law will obviously conflict with the Hamburg Rules.

In respect of Article 17.3 it may become necessary to adopt a broad interpretation of the words "intends to defraud" so as to ensure that only guarantees or undertakings given in a wilful intention of fraud will become invalid.

Article 18. Documents other than bills of lading

Article 18 deals with documents other than bills of lading issued by the carrier to evidence the receipt of the goods to be carried. The provision subjects those documents to the same evidentiary rules as are contained in Article 16.3 by stating that such documents are *prima facie* evidence of the conclusion of the contract and the taking over of the goods described in the documents.

PART V. CLAIMS AND ACTIONS

Article 19. Notice of loss, damage or delay

Notice of loss, damage or delay

Article 19 deals not only with notice by the consignee to the carrier for loss of or damage or delay to the goods (Article 19.1–19.6), but also with the carrier's notice of loss or damage to the shipper (Article 19.7).

This article provides that handing over of the goods by the carrier will be *prima facie* evidence of the delivery of the goods in good condition unless notice of loss or damage is given by the consignee not later than the working day after the day the goods were handed over to him. The notification has to specify the general nature of the loss or damage.

Article 19.1 specifies that the notice has to be given by the consignee. The notice may be addressed to the carrier (Article 19.1) the actual carrier (Article 19.6), or any other person acting on the carrier's or the actual carrier's behalf, including the master or the officer in charge (Article 19.8).

If the loss or damage is not apparent, Article 19.2 extends the period to 15 consecutive days after delivery. Article 19.2 also specifies a notice period of 60 consecutive days after delivery for a written notice for loss resulting from delay in delivery. Article 19.3 specifies that the notification has to be made in writing unless there has been a joint survey or inspection by the parties. Under Article 19.4

both parties must give all reasonable facilities to each other for inspecting and tallying the goods when there has been damage or loss.

Article 19.7 requires a carrier or actual carrier who suffers loss or damage attributable to the shipper to give written notice thereof to the shipper within 90 consecutive days after the occurrence which caused the loss or damage or after delivery of the goods to the consignee, whichever is the later. Failure to give such notice is *prima facie* evidence that the carrier or actual carrier suffered no loss or damage owing to the fault or neglect of the shipper, his servants or agents. This obligation imposed on the carrier balances the obligation of notice imposed on the consignee under Article 19.1. "Consecutive days" includes holidays and unifies the running of the period in different legal regimes with different national holidays.

Article 19.8 states that notice can be given to persons acting on behalf of the carrier, the actual carrier or the shipper, and that notices given to these persons are deemed to have been given to the carrier, the actual carrier or the shipper himself.

Article 20. Limitation of actions

Limitation of actions

Article 20.1 and 20.2 provide that actions relating to the carriage of goods under the Hamburg Rules are time-barred if judicial or arbitral proceedings have not been instituted within a period of two years from the day the goods were delivered or should have been delivered. Article 20.3 excludes the day on which the limitation period commences from the limitation period.

Under Article 20.5 a party held liable under the Hamburg Rules has an additional period of time after the expiration of the two-year period to institute an action for indemnity against another party who may be liable to him, if instituted within the time allowed by the law of the State where proceedings are instituted.

The two-year limitation period was adopted in the Hamburg Rules to safeguard the interests of the shipper, since the one-year period in the Hague Rules very often turned out to be too short in practice. The Hamburg Conference brought the time limit into line with that of some other transport conventions, e.g. the Athens Convention (Article 16) and the Warsaw Convention (Article 29) to safeguard the interests of the shipper. The Hamburg Rules contain additional relevant provisions. First, the limitation period is made clearly applicable not only to judicial but also to arbitral proceedings. Secondly, Article 20 specifies that the limitation period is not a prescription period but a time bar and therefore subject to suspension or interruption. Under the Hague Rules, national legal systems are not consistent in their treatment of the question whether the period is subject to suspension or interruption.

Although the Hamburg Conference did not agree on express rules concerning suspension and interruption of the limitation period, there will not necessarily be doubt on this issue. In practice, the most common basis for extending the period is the agreement of the person sued and this is expressly provided for in Article 20.4.

Article 21. Jurisdiction

Paragraph 1: Optional jurisdictions

Article 21 sets out a list of places where judicial proceedings, at the option of the plaintiff, may be instituted. Article 21.1 lists four places:

(a) the principal place of business or residence of the defendant; or

(b) the place where the contract was made, provided the defendant has a representative in that location; or

(c) the port of loading or discharge; or

(d) any additional place designated for that purpose in the contract.

Article 21.1(d) points out that these jurisdictions may be extended by contract. However, in accordance with Article 23, they may not be restricted by contract.

The courts mentioned in Article 21.1 do not derive their competence over a claim from the Hamburg Rules. Article 21.1 merely sets forth the jurisdictions in which a claim may be brought. The competence of a country's court depends on the national law of that country.

Jurisdiction in the sense of Article 21 refers to litigation on the merits of a claim. The rules concerning jurisdiction do not cover proceedings for provisional or protective measures which therefore may be brought anywhere if in accordance with applicable national law.

The Hamburg Conference debated whether or not the Convention should contain rules with respect to jurisdiction under the Convention. The majority were of the view that rules were necessary to protect the shipper against onerous jurisdiction clauses in bills of lading. Such clauses frequently require claims against the carrier to be brought in the place where he does business which may be far away from the claimant's location. Consequently, Article 21.1 stipulates several jurisdictions where the claim may be brought and leaves to the claimant the choice of bringing his claim in one of them. In addition, a uniform rule on jurisdiction was considered desirable because the validity and effect of jurisdiction clauses in bills of lading was uncertain and treated differently in various legal systems. These places are similar to those in Article 17 of the Athens Convention.[8] Included among the jurisdictions mentioned is any jurisdiction designated in the contract for carriage by sea. Thus, a certain flexibility is given to the parties to add additional jurisdictions beyond those specifically identified in the article. However, pursuant to Article 23, the optional jurisdictions available to a claimant may not be restricted by contract.

One purpose of unifying the law relating to the carriage of goods by sea is to eliminate the relative advantages of bringing a claim in a particular forum. However, the Hamburg Rules allow such a wide variety of optional jurisdictions that the forum shopping by the claimant is still possible, owing, for example, to differences in the size of awards, the time and cost of litigating, procedural rules or in the enforceability of awards.

8. Authors' footnote: Athens Convention, Convention relating to the Carriage of Passengers and their Luggage by Sea (Athens, 13 December 1974).

Paragraph 2: Arrest

In addition to the jurisdictions mentioned in Article 21.1 an action may be brought in the courts of a Contracting State where the carrying vessel or another vessel owned by the carrier is arrested. However, to protect the defendant the claimant is required to remove the litigation to one of the jurisdictions mentioned in Article 21.1 if the defendant so desires. There are shortcomings to such a requirement. As it is not technically possible for a claimant to remove his case from a court in one country to a court in another, he must withdraw his action in the jurisdiction where the vessel was arrested and institute new proceedings in the other jurisdiction.

Prior to the removal of the action the defendant must furnish sufficient security to ensure payment of any judgment awarded to the claimant. The sufficiency of the security will be determined by the court at the place of arrest. If the defendant does not ask for removal of the action, the court in the place of the arrest will remain competent. Permitting the action to be brought in the place of arrest only if it is located in a Contracting State is in contrast to Article 21.1, which does not require the places mentioned to be in Contracting States.

There may be a potential conflict between the jurisdiction provisions in the Hamburg Rules and those of the "Arrest Convention",[9] particularly Article 1(7) of that Convention. Participants in the Hamburg Conference were aware of the potential conflict and tried to keep it to an unavoidable minimum.

Paragraphs 3 and 4: Additional provisions

Article 21.3 and 21.4 provide additional procedural provisions supplementing the jurisdictional rules in Article 21.1 and 21.2.

Article 21.3 makes it clear that the jurisdictions mentioned in Article 21.1 and 21.2 are exclusive. The claimant may not bring a claim in any other jurisdiction. However, courts of a non-Contracting State cannot be bound by this rule except by virtue of the statement contained in the bill of lading pursuant to Article 23.3. Article 21.4(a) prohibits a new action on the same grounds between the same parties while litigation is pending in a competent court or when judgment has been delivered by such a court, unless the judgment is not enforceable in the country where the new claim has been brought. It is possible for a judgment issued in one country to be unenforceable in another because the Hamburg Rules do not provide for mutual enforcement of judgments. Article 21.4(b) and (c) mentions two procedures that are not to be considered as the starting of a new action: first, institution of measures with a view to obtaining enforcement of the earlier judgment; secondly, the removal of a case to a different court in the same country or to a court in another country in accordance with Article 21.2(a).

9. The International Convention for the Unification of Certain Rules relating to the Arrest of Sea-going Ships (Brussels, 10 May 1952).

Paragraph 5: Later agreement

Notwithstanding Article 21.1 and 21.2, Article 21.5 states that any agreement between the parties, after a claim has arisen, designating the place where the claimant may bring an action, is effective.

Therefore, parties may agree upon the bringing of an action in a jurisdiction other than one of those mentioned in Article 21.1 and 21.2. Under most national laws, such an agreement will be implied when both parties take part in the proceedings without claiming that the court lacks jurisdiction.

Article 22. Arbitration

Paragraphs 1 and 2: Principle

The Hamburg Rules deal with arbitration as an alternative to judicial proceedings. Article 22.1 provides that the parties may agree to submit their disputes under the Hamburg Rules to arbitration. Such an agreement must be in writing. Article 22.2 provides that an arbitration clause contained in a charterparty does not bind a third party who in good faith acquired the bill of lading issued under that charterparty, unless the bill of lading expressly refers to the arbitration clause.

Charterparties, unlike bills of lading, normally contain arbitration clauses. Under the present law the question of the effect of such clauses on transferees of a bill of lading issued pursuant to a charterparty is of great practical importance. Since the question is resolved differently in different national jurisdictions, Article 22.2 will contribute to a uniform resolution of this problem.

Paragraph 3: Place of arbitration

The Hamburg Rules require arbitration proceedings to be instituted, at the option of the claimant, in one of the places listed in Article 22.3. These places correspond with the places mentioned in Article 21.1, where judicial proceedings must be brought.

Article 22.3(b) refers to "any place designated", while Article 21.1(d) refers to "any additional place designated". Although this drafting difference might cause uncertainty, it is clear from the context of Article 22.3 that the wording intended is that of Article 21.1(d), i.e. "any additional place designated". Comparable to Article 21.5, Article 22.6 provides that nothing in Article 22 affects the validity of an agreement relating to arbitration made after a claim has arisen.

Paragraph 4: Application of the Hamburg Rules

Article 22.4 requires the arbitration tribunal to apply the Hamburg Rules. That provision is supplemented by Article 22.5, which provides that the provisions of Article 22.3 and 22.4 shall be deemed part of every arbitration clause or agreement.

Paragraphs 5 and 6: Additional provisions

The two last paragraphs of Article 22 contain some additional rules. Article 22.5, as already mentioned, deems the rules of Article 22.3 and 22.4 to be part of every arbitration clause even if not so agreed and expressly stated. By virtue of Article 23.3 the rules of Article 22.3 and 22.4 are deemed to be in the agreement even when not considered by the parties.

Like Article 21.5, Article 22.6 provides for freedom of agreement regarding arbitration when the agreement is made after the claim has arisen.

PART VI. SUPPLEMENTARY PROVISIONS

Article 23. Contractual stipulations

Paragraphs 1 and 2: Mandatory rules

Articles 23.1 makes null and void any stipulation in the contract of carriage or transport document that derogates directly or indirectly from the obligations under the Convention. Article 23.2 leaves open, however, the possibility of increasing the carrier's liability.

Article 23.1 expressly states that the nullity of a stipulation in a contract of carriage or transport document does not affect the validity of other provisions of the contract or document. This resolves a question that is unclear under the Hague-Visby Rules. Article 23.1 expressly renders one type of clause null and void: a clause assigning to the carrier the benefit of any insurance on the goods.

Paragraph 3: Statement of application of the Convention

Article 23.3 requires the bill of lading or other document evidencing the contract of carriage to state that the carriage is subject to the provisions of the Hamburg Rules which nullify any stipulation derogating therefrom to the detriment of the shipper or consignee. The aims of this provision are twofold. First, to make the shipper aware that the contract of carriage is governed by the Hamburg Rules, and secondly to foster the application of the Hamburg Rules even in non-Contracting States.

Paragraph 4: Indemnity

Under Article 23.4 the carrier must compensate a claimant who incurs loss as a result of the omission of the statement referred to in Article 23.3 or the insertion of stipulations which are null and void under Article 23.1. The loss may be caused by the claimant's having been misled by an incorrect insertion in the bill of lading or by the failure of a court in a non-Contracting State to apply the Hamburg Rules when it would have done so if the statement had been inserted.

Article 23.4 was adopted by the Hamburg Conference because it felt that the cargo interests were often misled into claiming against carriers or were discouraged from bringing such claims by clauses in bills of lading that were in fact null and void under the applicable law.

Article 24. General average

Article 24.1 allows the application of provisions in the contract of carriage by sea or in national law regarding the adjustment of general average.

Article 24.2 provides that, with the exception of the rules set forth in Article 20 concerning the limitation period, the provisions of the Hamburg Rules relating to the liability of the carrier for loss or damage to the goods also determine whether the consignee may refuse contribution in general average, and the liability of the carrier to indemnify a consignee who has made contribution or paid salvage. Thus, if the carrier is liable to the shipper under the Hamburg Rules for loss of or damage to the goods, the carrier may not ask for contribution and security in general average.

Although Article 24.2 maintains the traditional relationship between the contract of carriage and general average, it may produce some changes. For example, if the consignee is asked to contribute in general average he will in practice be required to provide a bond before taking delivery of his cargo, even though he may be entitled to claim damage from the carrier (cf. rule D of the 1974 York-Antwerp Rules[10]). Owing to the changed liability system, more situations may occur under the Hamburg Rules than under the Hague Rules when the carrier will be liable (e.g., because he can no longer claim the defence of "error in navigation") and thus will be unable to obtain contributions from the consignee.

Article 25. Other Conventions

Article 25.1 states that the Hamburg rules do not modify the rights or duties of the carrier, actual carrier and their servants and agents provided for in international conventions or national laws relating to the limitation of liability of owners of seagoing ships.

At present, the right to limit the liability is governed by the Brussels Convention, the London Convention or similar national legislation.

The Hamburg Conference decided that the Hamburg Rules should be subordinate even to national laws permitting a carrier to invoke an overall limit of liability because the right to do so is accepted worldwide. It should be noted, however, that national laws may provide for very low limitation sums.

Paragraph 2: Mandatory provisions of other conventions

Article 25.2 states that the provisions on jurisdiction and arbitration (Articles 21 and 22) do not prevent the application of the mandatory provisions of other exist-

10. Rule D of the York-Antwerp Rules states: "Rights to contribution in general average shall not be affected, though the event which gave rise to the sacrifice or expenditure may have been due to the fault of one of the parties to the adventure, but this shall not prejudice any remedies or defences which may be open against or to that party in respect of such fault."

ing multilateral conventions on those subjects, if the disputes involved are exclusively between the parties having their principal place of business in Contracting States of the other Conventions. An example of such a Convention is the "Arbitral Awards Convention".[11] Because these Conventions deal with matters of procedure rather than substance, the application of the Hamburg Rules to a dispute covered by those Conventions (e.g., pursuant to Article 22.4 of the Hamburg Rules) would not conflict with the provisions of those Conventions.

Paragraph 3: Nuclear damage

Pursuant to Article 25.3, no liability arises under the Hamburg Rules for damage caused by a nuclear incident if the operator of the nuclear installation is liable either by virtue of two specifically named international Conventions or by national law equally as favourable to the victims of such incidents as those two Conventions. The reason for this provision is that losses arising from nuclear damage are normally much higher than losses usually suffered under the carriage of goods by sea, and the provisions of the international Conventions and national laws dealing with liability for nuclear damage are better suited than the Hamburg Rules to the protection of victims of nuclear incidents.

Paragraph 4: Liability for loss, damage or delay to luggage

Article 25.4 provides that no liability shall arise under the Hamburg Rules in respect of luggage for which the carrier is responsible under an international Convention or national law relating to the carriage of passengers and their luggage by sea. This provision was required because luggage is very often considered to be goods. It is more appropriate for passenger luggage to be covered by Conventions such as the Athens Convention (under which the limits of liability are considerably higher than in the Hamburg rules) or by national law specifically relating to passenger luggage, rather than by the Hamburg Rules.

Paragraph 5: Other Conventions already in force

Article 25.5 states that nothing in the Hamburg Rules prevents a Contracting State from applying any other existing international Convention which applies mandatorily to contracts of carriage of goods primarily by modes of transport other than transport by sea as well as to future revisions or amendments of those Conventions. Conventions such as the CMR would be covered by this article, as would COTIF — Appendix CIM,[12] as a revision of the CIM. The carrier's liability under those conventions is much greater than under the Hamburg Rules.

11. The Recognition and Enforcement of Foreign Arbitral Awards Convention, New York, 10 June 1958.

12. COTIF — Appendix CIM: Uniform Rules concerning the Contract for International Transport by Rail (CIM), Appendix B to the Convention concerning International Transport by Rail (COTIF) (Bern, 9 May 1980).

Article 26. Unit of account

Article 26 provides that the unit of account to be used in the Rules to express the limits of liability is, in most cases, the SDR of the International Monetary Fund. This is, at present, the most satisfactory unit of account for expressing financial amounts which are to have worldwide application.

Article 26.2 provides a special rule for those States that are not members of the International Monetary Fund and whose national laws do not allow them to calculate the limits of liability by reference to the SDR. Those States may fix the limits of liability applicable in their territory in Franc Poincaré.[13]

This is the same unit of account found in Article IV, rule 5(d) of the Hague-Visby Rules and in Article II of the 1979 Protocol. The Franc Poincaré is based on a defined amount and fineness of gold; however, there is no longer a fixed relationship between national currencies and gold. Therefore, the Hamburg Rules, in Article 26.4, leave it to the Contracting States' discretion to convert the amounts expressed in Franc Poincaré into their national currency in such a manner as to correspond as closely as possible to the same real value for the liability limits set forth in Article 6 of the Hamburg Rules.

PART VII. FINAL CLAUSES

Most modern Conventions are done in more than one language or in one language with an official translation.

For example, the London Convention is in English, French, Russian and Spanish. The Athens Convention is in English and French with official translations into Russian and Spanish.

It has been argued that this multitude of languages may complicate the application of the Convention. However, this argument can equally well be used against other multi-language Conventions.

Bearing in mind the various legal and linguistic systems and terms which the languages represent, some divergences between the language versions are unavoidable.

The question will arise as to how those divergences can be resolved.

A possible solution may be found in Article 33.4 of the Vienna Convention on the Law of Treaties (Vienna, 23 May 1969) which states that "when a comparison of the authentic texts discloses a difference of meaning which the application of Articles 31 and 32 [the general interpretation rules] do not remove, the meaning which best reconciles the texts, having regard to the object and purpose of the treaty, shall be adopted". Article 32 of the Vienna Convention provides that, if the text permits more than one interpretation, courts have to look at the preparatory

13. Authors' footnote: The Franc Poincaré is an imaginary unit equal to 65.5 milligrammes of gold of 900/1000 fineness. The rate of exchange is set by Orders in Council frequently amending the sterling equivalent to the Franc Poincaré. For claims in the UK the rate of exchange applicable to the date of settlement applies and not the date when the claim arose.

work; if this does not provide a solution, they must look to the purpose of the Convention to provide a reasonable interpretation. In addition to those provisions, Article 3 of the Hamburg Rules, which stresses the need for uniformity in interpretation, will assist in resolving divergences among the different language versions.

APPENDIX 7

CARGO CONVENTIONS (COMPARISON OF HAGUE/HAGUE-VISBY AND HAMBURG RULES)

1. Which voyages covered?
2. Which contracts covered?
3. Geographical application
4. Who is the carrier?
5. Contract and tort claims
6. Carrier's general duty of care
7. Carrier's defences
8. Burden of proof
9. Fire
10. Live animals
11. Deck cargo
12. Dangerous cargo
13. Limits of liability
14. Loss of right to limit liability
15. Lower limits by agreement?
16. Higher limits by agreement?
17. Deviation
18. What information must the bill contain?
19. What is the effect of statements in the bill?
20. Duties of shipper in supplying carrier with information
21. Letters of indemnity
22. Notification of damage
23. Consequences of failing to notify carrier of loss under 22 above.
24. Limitation of action
25. Where can cargo owner commence proceedings?
26. Arbitration
27. General average
28. Provisions which conflict with the Rules

November 1992

	Hague Rules	*Hague-Visby Rules*	*Hamburg Rules*
1. Which voyages covered?	Rules are silent.	Art X (a) Bill issued in a contracting state (b) carriage from contracting state	Art 2 (a) Bill issued in contracting state (b) carriage from contracting state

		Hague Rules	*Hague-Visby Rules*	*Hamburg Rules*
			(c) contract of carriage expressly applies Rules	(c) carriage to contracting state (d) Bill provides Rules are to apply
2.	Which contracts covered?	Art I(b) Bill of lading or "other similar document of title". Not charterparties.	Art I(b) Same as Hague Rules.	Art 1.6 Contract of carriage by sea. Need not be a bill or document of title. Not charterparties.
3.	Geographical application	Art I(e) "covers the period from the time when the goods are loaded on to the time when they are discharged from the ship". Tackle to tackle.	Art I(e) Same as Hague Rules.	Art 4 Carrier is responsible while in "charge" of the goods at the port of loading, during the carriage, and at the port of discharge, i.e. normally from time taken over from shipper to time delivered to consignee, subject to local port regulations.
4.	Who is the carrier?	Art I(a) Owner or charterer "who enters into contract of carriage with a shipper".	Art I(a) Same as Hague Rules.	Art 1.1, Art 10, Art 11 "any person by whom or in whose name a contract of carriage has been concluded with a shipper". Covers "actual" and "contractual" carrier.
5.	Contract and tort claims	Rules are silent. May apply to just contract claims. Applies to both under English law.	Art IV *bis* Apply to contract and tort claims.	Art 7 Apply to contract and tort claims.
6.	Carrier's general duty of care	Art III 1. Carrier must exercise due diligence before and at beginning of voyage to: (a) make ship seaworthy	Art III Same as Hague Rules.	Art 5.1 Carrier, his servants and agents, must take all measures that could reasonably be required to avoid the event causing loss and its consequences.

	Hague Rules	*Hague-Visby Rules*	*Hamburg Rules*
	(b) properly man, equip and supply the ship (c) make holds etc. fit and safe for reception, carriage and preservation of cargo 2. Carrier must properly and carefully load, handle, stow, carry, keep, care for and discharge goods carried.		
7. Carrier's defences	Art IV 1. Unseaworthiness—only defence is for carrier to show he exercised "due diligence" to ensure vessel seaworthy before and at beginning of voyage. 2. Properly and carefully load etc. The following defences apply: (a) Act, neglect, or default of the master, mariner, pilot or the servants of the carrier in the navigation or in the management of the ship (b) Fire, unless caused by the actual fault or privity of the carrier (c) Perils, dangers and accidents of the sea or other navigable waters (d) Act of God (e) Act of war (f) Act of public enemies	Art IV Same as Hague Rules.	Art 5.1 Carrier must prove he, his servants or agents, took all measures that could reasonably be required to avoid the occurrence and its consequences.

	Hague Rules	Hague-Visby Rules	Hamburg Rules
	(g) Arrest or restraint of princes, rulers or people, or seizure under legal process (h) Quarantine restrictions (i) Act or omission of the shipper, or owner of the goods, his agent or representative (j) Strikes or lock-outs, or stoppage or restraint of labour from whatever cause, whether partial or general (k) Riots and civil commotions (l) Saving or attempting to save life or property at sea (m) Wastage in bulk or weight or any other loss or damage arising from inherent defect, quality or vice of the goods (n) Insufficiency of packing (o) Insufficiency or inadequacy of marks (p) Latent defects not discoverable by due diligence (o) Any other cause arising without the actual fault or privity of the carrier, or without the fault or neglect of the agents or servants of the carrier, but the		

	Hague Rules	*Hague-Visby Rules*	*Hamburg Rules*
	burden of proof shall be on the person claiming the benefit of this exception to show that neither the actual fault or privity of the carrier nor the fault or neglect of the agents or servants of the carrier contributed to the loss or damage.		
8. Burden of proof	Rules are unclear (except under Art IV(2)(q)). Under English law cargo owner must establish inference of unseaworthiness or failure to properly and carefully carry the goods, and then carrier must prove relevant defence in 7.	Same as Hague Rules.	Carrier must prove that reasonable steps to avoid loss were taken unless damage is caused by fire (see 9 below).
9. Fire	Arts III & IV If due to e.g. poor stowage, carrier only liable if caused by his actual fault or privity. If caused by unseaworthiness, carrier liable unless he exercised due diligence to ensure vessel seaworthy before and at beginning of voyage.	Arts III & IV Same as Hague Rules.	Art 5.4 Carrier liable if claimant proves fire arose from fault or neglect on the part of the carrier, his servants or agents.
10. Live animals	Art I(c) Excluded from Rules.	Art I(c) Same as Hague Rules. C/f UK COGSA 1971, S1(7) which applies Rules to live animals.	Arts 1.5 & 5.5 Rules apply but carrier not liable for inherent "special risks". If carrier complies with shipper's instructions

	Hague Rules	*Hague-Visby Rules*	*Hamburg Rules*
			he will be presumed not to be liable.
11. Deck cargo	Art I(c) Excluded from Rules if stated to be carried on deck.	Art I(c) Same as Hague Rules. C/f UK COGSA 1971, S1(7) which applies Rules to deck cargo (see e.g. *Chanda* [1989] 2 Lloyd's Rep. 494).	Art 9 Rules do not exclude deck cargo. Carrier can undertake deck carriage if agreed with shipper or accords with the "usage of a particular trade or is required by statutory rules or regulations". Must be statement in Bill that goods carried on deck. Failure to agree deck carriage makes carrier liable for damage, loss or delay, resulting solely from carriage on deck. Carrier cannot limit liability when deck carriage is in breach of express agreement to carry below deck.
12. Dangerous cargo	Art IV Rule 6 Inflammable, explosive or dangerous goods if loaded without knowledge of the master (or carrier's agent) may be discharged, rendered harmless or destroyed at shipper's expense. If carrier knows of their nature but they prove dangerous they may still be discharged, rendered harmless or destroyed without liability on the part of the carrier, save in general average.	Art IV Rule 6 Same as Hague Rules.	Art 13 Similar provisions apply, and the shipper is obliged to mark and label dangerous goods in a suitable manner.

	Hague Rules	*Hague-Visby Rules*	*Hamburg Rules*
13. Limits of liability (a) Goods lost or damaged	Art IV Rule 5 £100 per package or unit unless value declared and inserted in bill of lading.	Art IV Rule 5 10,000 Poincaré Francs per package or unit or 30 Poincaré Francs per kilo of gross weight of damaged or lost goods whichever is higher. By virtue of SDR Protocol 1979 2 SDRs per kg or 666.67 SDRs per package.	Art 6 2.5 SDRs per kg or 835 SDRs per package or shipping unit.
(b) Goods delayed	No special provisions.	Same as Hague Rules.	Art 6 2.5 × freight payable on goods delayed, subject to upper limit of total freight on all goods or amount of limitation if goods have been lost or destroyed under formula in (a) above.
14. Loss of right to limit liability	No special provisions but carrier's liability may be unlimited if unjustified deviation, or deck carriage.	Art IV Rule 5(e) Right to limit lost if carrier intends to cause loss or is reckless knowing loss would probably result. May also be lost if unjustified deviation or deck carriage.	Art 8 Carrier will only lose right to limit liability if he intended to cause loss or was reckless knowing such loss would probably result. Deck carriage where expressly prohibited will result in loss of right to limit liability.
15. Lower limits by agreement?	Art VI Only permitted where not an ordinary shipment, and reasonable in special circumstances.	Art VI Same as Hague Rules.	No specific right to agree lower limits.
16. Higher limits by agreement?	Art V Permitted if recorded in Bill.	Art V Same as Hague Rules.	Art 6.4 Art 15 Permitted if agreed Should be recorded in Bill.

	Hague Rules	*Hague-Visby Rules*	*Hamburg Rules*
17. Deviation	Deviating carrier might lose right to rely on defences in Rules and lose right to limit liability. Art IV Rule 4 provides "any deviation in saving or attempting to save life or property at sea, or any reasonable deviation shall not be deemed to be an infringement or breach of the Rules or contract of carriage".	Same as Hague Rules.	No special provisions. Deviation if it caused loss is subject to general test of carrier's liability Art 5.6 exempts a carrier from liability where he attempts to save life or "reasonable measures" are taken to save property. This would apply to deviation as much as any other cause of loss.
18. What information must the Bill contain?	Art III Rule 3 (a) leading marks necessary for identifying goods. (b) number of packages or pieces, *or* the quantity or weight, as the case may be, as furnished by the shipper.	Art III Rule 3 Same as Hague Rules.	Art 15 (a) the general nature of the goods, the leading marks necessary for identification of the goods, an express statement, if applicable, as to the dangerous character of the goods, the number of packages or pieces, *and* the weight of the goods or their quantity otherwise expressed, all such particulars as furnished by the shipper. (b) the apparent condition of the goods. (c) the name and principal place of business of the carrier. (d) the name of the shipper.

Hague Rules	*Hague-Visby Rules*	*Hamburg Rules*
		(e) the consignee if named by shipper. (f) the port of loading under the contract of carriage by sea and the date on which the goods were taken over by the carrier at the port of loading. (g) the port of discharge under the contract of carriage by sea. (h) the number of originals of the bill of lading, if more than one. (i) the place of issuance of the bill of lading. (j) the signature of the carrier or a person acting on his behalf. (k) freight to the extent payable by the consignee. (l) the statement referred to in paragraph 3 of Art 23, i.e. applicability of the Convention. (m) statement if applicable, that the goods shall or may be carried on deck. (n) the date or the period of delivery of the goods at the port of discharge if expressly agreed upon between the parties.

	Hague Rules	*Hague-Visby Rules*	*Hamburg Rules*
			(o) any increased limit or limits of liability where agreed. *If the carrier is unable to state any of the matters in (a) above he should express his omission in the Bill.*
19. What is the effect of statements in the Bill?	Art III Rule 4 *Prima facie* evidence of their accuracy.	Art III Rule 4 *Prima facie* evidence in hands of shipper, conclusive in hands of third party, e.g. consignee to whom Bill is transferred in good faith.	Art 16 *Prima facie* evidence of statement in hands of shipper (whether shipped or received Bill). Conclusive in hand of third party who relies on statements. However, if freight is payable by holder of Bill failure to state this is evidence that no freight is payable.
20. Duties of shipper in supplying carrier with information	Art III Rule 5 Shipper is deemed to guarantee accuracy of statements as to weight and quantity of cargo. Shipper to indemnify carrier for loss resulting from errors.	Art III Rule 5 Same as Hague Rules.	Art 17 Same as Hague Rules.
21. Effectiveness of letter of indemnity issued by shipper for carrier not clausing Bill	No specific provisions Void under English Law (*Brown Jenkinson & Co Ltd* v. *Percy Dalton (Ldn) Ltd* [1957] 2 QB 621).	Same as Hague Rules.	Art 17 Void for bill in hands of consignee. Valid against shipper unless carrier intended to defraud consignee. If fraud, carrier may not limit liability.
22. Notification of damage	Art III Rule 6 Notice of loss or damage must be given in writing to the carrier or his	Art III Rule 6 Same as Hague Rules.	Art 19 Notice of loss or damage to be given in writing to carrier: (i) by working day

	Hague Rules	Hague-Visby Rules	Hamburg Rules
	agent: (i) on day of delivery or (ii) within three days where damage is latent.		following delivery to consignee, or (ii) within 15 days of delivery where damage is latent Notice of delay must be given within 60 days of delivery. Carrier must give notice to shipper of complaint within 90 days of delivery.
23. Consequences of failing to notify carrier of loss, damage or delay under 22 above	Art III Rule 6 *Prima facie* evidence of delivery of goods in condition described by Bill.	Art III Rule 6 Same as Hague Rules.	Art 19 *Prima facie* evidence of delivery of goods in condition described by Bill. If goods delayed and complaint not made within 60 days the carrier is exempted from liability.
24. Limitation of action	Art III Rule 6 "Suit" must be brought within one year of delivery or date delivery should have taken place.	Art III Rule 6 Same as Hague Rules. Art III Rule 6 *bis* Indemnity actions may be brought after one year, the period for commencing suit to be not less than 15 months after discharge.	Art 20 Litigation or arbitration to be commenced within two years from date of delivery of goods or the last day upon which goods should have been delivered. Indemnity proceedings may be commenced after this period (at least 90 days from date of commencement of action against carrier must be allowed).
25. Where can cargo owner commence proceedings?	Rules are silent.	Same as Hague Rules.	Art 21 May sue in court of: (a) Principal place of business of carrier (b) place contract was made (c) port of loading

	Hague Rules	*Hague-Visby Rules*	*Hamburg Rules*
			(d) port of discharge (e) place designated by contract of carriage (f) place of arrest of vessel, may be challenged by the carrier, if he submits to one of the other jurisdictions and provides security for the claim.
26. Arbitration	Rules are silent.	Same as Hague Rules.	Art 22 Arbitration agreement permitted. If incorporating charterparty arbitration clause, must be comprised in bill of lading as "special annotation". Claimant may choose where to commence arbitration from: (a) place where defendant has principal place of business (b) place where contract was made (c) port of loading (d) port of discharge (e) place specified in arbitration clause.
27. General average	Art V "Nothing in these rules shall be held to present the insertion in a Bill of any lawful provision regarding general average".	Art V Same as Hague Rules.	Art 24 "The provisions of this Convention relating to the liability of the carrier for loss of or damage to the goods also determine whether the consignee may

	Hague Rules	*Hague-Visby Rules*	*Hamburg Rules*
			refuse contribution in general average ..."
28. Provisions which conflict with the Rules	Art III Rule 8 Void.	Art III Rule 8 Void.	Art 23.1 Void and compensation may be payable where claimant has suffered a loss: see Art 23.4.

APPENDIX 8

CASE STUDIES (COMPARISON OF OUTCOMES UNDER HAGUE/HAGUE-VISBY AND HAMBURG RULES)

From a paper prepared by Frances M Hannah of the Queensland University of Technology on behalf of the Australian Chamber of Shipping

Case name	*Issue(s)*	*Outcome under Hague/Hague-Visby Rules*	*Outcome under Hamburg Rules*
The Hellenic Dolphin [1978] 2 Lloyd's Rep. 336	(a) latent defect—Art IV(2)(p) (b) perils of the sea—Art IV(2)(c) (c) defence applies unless plaintiff can show unseaworthiness	The plaintiffs could not show failure to exercise due diligence. Therefore, Art IV(2)(p) applied to relieve the defendants of liability.	Art IV(2)(p) is not available under the Hamburg Rules. Onus of proof is on the carrier to show all reasonable measures were taken. On these facts, they were, but again this would need to be tested.
Shipping Corporation of India Ltd v. *Gamlen Chemical Co (A Asia) Pty Ltd* (1980) 55 ALJR 88 See also: *Great China Metal Ind Co Ltd* v. *International Shipping Corp Berhad* (1993, unreported)	(a) perils of the sea—Art IV Rule 2(c) of Hague Rules (b) unseaworthiness	Art IV Rule 2(c) did not apply because the loss or damage to cargo could have been avoided by reasonable care on the part of the carrier. Art III Rule 2 applied because inadequate storage was the principal cause of the loss.	The Hamburg Rules Article 5(1) also require reasonable measures by the carrier. Would the outcome be the same? Perhaps, but the absence of the Art III & IV wording would lead to litigation on this point.
Chubu Asahi Cotton Spinning Co v. *The Tenos* (1986) 12 FLR 291	Art IV Rule 2(a) of Hague Rules—the navigation defence	The damage which occurred was not related to the management of the ship. Thus, Art IV Rule 2(a) was not available to relieve the carriers of liability.	This contentious defence has not been included in the Hamburg Rules. The outcome would probably be the same on these facts, applying Art 5(1).
Minnesota Mining & Manufacturing (Aust) Ltd v. *The Novoaltaisk* [1972] 2 NSWLR 47	(a) Art III Rule 1(a) Hague Rules (b) Art IV Rule 2(a)	The Art IV Rule 2(a) exception applied because the damage was done in the course of the management of the ship.	The Hamburg Rules would doubtless give a more favourable outcome for the cargo-owner here.

Case name	*Issue(s)*	*Outcome under Hague/Hague-Visby Rules*	*Outcome under Hamburg Rules*
Brown Boveri (Australia) Pty Ltd v. *Baltic Shipping Co* [1989] 1 Lloyd's Rep. 518	(a) limitation of liability (b) package/unit limitation (c) meaning of £100 per unit in Art IV Rule 5 and Art IX of the Hague Rules	The per package limitation was interpreted as meaning £100 gold value at present prices for each package or unit *viz*. $32,221.33 in total, instead of £200 stg. in total.	The Hamburg Rules, Art. 6 Rule 1 allow 835 SDRs per package or 2.5 SDRs per kilogramme. At (about) $A2 per SDR, this is a much less favourable outcome for cargo-owners.
PS Chellaram & Co Ltd v. *China Ocean Shipping Co* [1991] 1 Lloyd's Rep. 493	(a) application of Rules (b) limitation of liability (c) illegibility of bill of lading	The applicability of the Rules was much broader than the Rules seemed to state, including events after discharge of the goods. Illegibility of the bill of lading did not affect its validity.	The Hamburg Rules have nothing further to offer here. The Hague-Visby Rules can be just as effective.
Kenya Railways v. *Antares Co Pty Ltd*, (*The Antares*) (Nos 1 & 2) [1987] 1 Lloyd's Rep. 424	(a) deck cargo (b) time limit of one year under Hague-Visby Rules (Art III, Rule 6)	The time limit for bringing of actions, under the Hague-Visby Rules applied compulsorily. The deck cargo issue did not entitle the time limit to be extended.	The Hamburg Rules in Art 20 Rule 1 give limitation period of two years. The plaintiff would have benefited from this provision on these facts, and thus the Hamburg Rules would have favoured the shipper here.
The Captain Gregos [1990] 1 Lloyd's Rep. 310	(a) time bar in Hague-Visby Rules Art III Rule 6 (b) misdelivery	The time bar applied absolutely to prevent the plaintiff from recovering.	The Hamburg Rules in Art 20 Rule 1 give a limitation period of two years. The plaintiff would have benefited from this provision on these facts, and thus the Hamburg Rules would have favoured the shipper here.
J Gadsen Pty Ltd v. *Australian Coastal Shipping Commission* [1977] 1 NSWLR 575	(a) time bar in Hague Rules (b) documentation necessary	The time bar in Art III Rule 6 did not apply, because the owner had not issued a bill of lading.	The time bar in the Hamburg Rules would have applied here, since there was a delay of three years. Documentation would then be irrelevant, even though the Hamburg Rules do not require the issue of a bill of lading. This would result in a less favourable outcome for the cargo-owner.

Case name	*Issue(s)*	*Outcome under Hague/Hague-Visby Rules*	*Outcome under Hamburg Rules*
The Chanda [1989] 2 Lloyd's Rep. 494	(a) deck cargo (b) limitation of liability under Hague Rules (c) package limitation under West German commercial code	The carriage of the cargo on deck was unauthorised. The carrier could not limit liability under the relevant law in these circumstances.	The Hamburg Rules would give the same outcome—Arts 5(1), 8(1) and 9(1). However, this does not take into account the probable need for interpretation of all three of these paragraphs.
The Morviken [1983] 1 Lloyd's Rep. 1	(a) exclusive jurisdiction clause (b) stay of action (c) package limitation	The Hague-Visby Rules applied despite a choice of law clause in the bill of lading to the contrary. Art III Rule 8 overrode the bill of lading clause. Thus, the UK was the correct forum and English Law applied. This was a policy decision by the House of Lords.	The COGSA 1991 sections on jurisdiction would give a similar outcome, whether the Hague-Visby or Hamburg Rules applied. The only contentious issue here would be the applicability of the doctrine of *forum non conveniens* and its effect on our choice of rules under COGSA 1991.
The Komninos S [1991] 1 Lloyd's Rep. 370	(a) proper law of contract (b) whether Hague-Visby Rules applied to limit liability of carrier	English law was the proper law of the contract. The Hague-Visby Rules did not apply, however, because of Art X(a)	Could the Hamburg Rules be made to apply if Australian Law was the proper law, but the goods were shipped from a non-Hamburg Rules country? Yes, under Art 2(1)(b). However, again the doctrine of *forum non conveniens* could affect this outcome.
Wilson v. *Compagnie des Messageries Maritimes* [1954] 2 Lloyd's Rep. 544	(a) jurisdiction of Australian Courts (b) stay of action because of incorrect forum	No ousting of jurisdiction of Australian courts was allowed under Sea Carriage of Goods Act 1924, s.9(2).	The same effect is provided for in s.11(2) COGSA 1991. The Rules applicable do not affect this outcome.
Furness Withy (Australia) Pty Ltd v. *Metal Distributors (UK) Ltd (The Amazonia)* [1990] 1 Lloyd's Rep. 236	(a) proper law of contract (b) arbitration clause	The parties' mutual intention was that English law and arbitration should apply, but the written agreement in fact specified Australian Law as applicable.	The exclusive jurisdiction provided for in s.11 (1) and (2) of COGSA 1991 seems also to apply to arbitration. The choice of Rules is probably irrelevant here.

Case name	*Issue(s)*	*Outcome under Hague/Hague-Visby Rules*	*Outcome under Hamburg Rules*
Maxine Footwear Co Ltd v. *Canadian Government Merchant Marine Ltd* [1959] AC 589	(a) Hague Rules Art III Rule1 — seaworthiness (b) Art IV Rule 2(b) — fire defence	Article III Rule 1 applied while the ship was in port and after loading had begun. The ship was rendered unseaworthy by lack of due diligence by the carrier.	The Hamburg Rules Arts 4 and 5(1) would probably give the same outcome, but this would be difficult to judge without litigation. The fire defence in Art 5(4)(a) has been retained with (probably) added confusion.
The Muncaster Castle [1961] 1 Lloyd's Rep 57	The meaning of "exercise due diligence to make a ship seaworthy" in the Hague/Hague-Visby Rules.	The meaning of these words is that "a carrier was responsible to a cargo-owner unless due diligence in the work has been shown by every person to whom any part of the necessary work has been entrusted".	These words do not appear in the Hamburg Rules Art 5(1). "All measures that could reasonably be required" would need to be tested in the courts.
Pyrene Company Ltd v. *Scindia Steam Navigation Co Ltd* [1954] 1 Lloyd's Rep. 321	(a) applicability of Rules to handling of goods before loading. (b) Hague Rules Art I(b), (c) (c) limitation of liability by carrier	The application of the Rules is dependent on the nature of the contract between the parties. The Rules do not operate independently.	The Hamburg Rules apply more broadly than "tackle-to-tackle", but the nature of the underlying contract is still paramount. Therefore this issue would still require litigation.
Mayhew Foods Ltd v. *Overseas Containers Ltd* [1984] 1 Lloyd's Rep. 317	(a) applicability of the Rules to damage suffered in a non-sea segment of a carriage (b) limitation of liability by carrier	The contract overrode the Hague-Visby Rules (as contained in COGSA 1971 (UK)) in applying to a port-to-port carriage including transhipment.	There is no advantage in applying the Hamburg Rules if the Hague-Visby Rules can also be applied port-to-port by contract.
The Anders Maersk [1986] 1 Lloyd's Rep. 483	(a) the essential nature of the contract between the parties (b) applicability of COGSA 1936 (US) *vs* COGSA 1971 (UK) (c) limitation of liability by the carrier	The Hague-Visby Rules did not apply. COGSA 1936 (US) did apply, and limited liability of the carrier to $US 1,000.	The Hamburg Rules would not apply either on similar facts to override COGSA 1936 (US). Therefore, the Hamburg Rules would present no advantage.
Svenska Traktor v. *Maritime Agencies (Southampton) Ltd* [1953] 2 Lloyd's Rep. 124	(a) deck cargo (b) liberty clause re deck cargo in bill of lading. (c) application of Art	Shipowners were entitled to carry goods on deck, but subject always to Art III Rule 2. They had failed to	The Hamburg Rules cover deck cargo, but it is difficult to see a different outcome given Art 5, Rule 1.

Case name	*Issue(s)*	*Outcome under Hague/Hague-Visby Rules*	*Outcome under Hamburg Rules*
	III Rule 2 of the Hague Rules	fulfil the Art III Rule 2 obligation. There were no Art IV Rule 2 defences.	Art 9 is so confusingly drafted that it will have to be interpreted by the Courts to discover its meaning (if any). The applicability of Art 8 Rule 1 would also have to be tested.
Encyclopedia Britannica Inc v. *The "Hong Kong Producer" and Universal Marine Corporation* [1969] 2 Lloyd's Rep. 536	(a) deck cargo (b) COGSA 1936 (US) application (c) short form bill of lading as a contractual document	The short-form bill of lading incorporated the terms of the regular contract. However, the carrier was liable in full since the stowing of containers on deck was unreasonable deviation.	The Hamburg Rules cover deck cargo. The wording of Art 9 Rule 1 reflects the defendant's contention in this case. Therefore, there would be no advantage in applying the Hamburg Rules on similar facts, since the plaintiff recovered in full.
Stag Line Ltd v. *Foscolo Mango and Co Ltd* [1932] AC 328	Deviation-Hague Rules Art IV Rule 4	The deviation was not reasonable, and the carrier was liable.	Hamburg Rules Art 5 Rule 6 would probably give the same outcome, although it is narrower than the Hague-Visby deviation provision.
The Ardennes [1951] 1 KB 55	(a) deviation (b) bill of lading as evidence of contract	The deviation caused delay which resulted in liability for the shipowner. The bill of lading was not in itself the contract between shipper and ship-owner, so that oral terms were admissible.	Again, the outcome should be the same under the Hamburg Rules.
Comalco Aluminium Ltd v. *Mogal Freight Service Pty Ltd* (1993) 113 ALR 377	(a) documentation required by Rules (b) Hague Rules application (c) exclusion clauses	A consignment note was the principal document involved. The consignment note had the characteristics of a bill of lading and so could be designated as such. There was no liability under the Hague Rules because exclusion clauses operated effectively to avoid liability for inadequate packing.	If the document can be characterised as a bill of lading, the Hamburg Rules offer no extra benefit on these facts. If the contract is wider than the Rules, the Hamburg Rules will not override exclusion clauses either.

INDEX